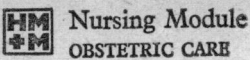

Nursing Module
OBSTETRIC CARE

SERIES EDITOR
Kathleen M. Berry, SRN SCM RNT AcDipEd

In the same series
Psychiatric Care
Community Care
Geriatric Care

HM+M Nursing Modules

Obstetric Care

Betty R. Sweet, SRN SCM MTD DN LondPtA
Tutor in Charge, British Hospital
for Mothers and Babies, Woolwich, London

Irene F. Cape, SRN SCM MTD
formerly Midwifery Tutor,
British Hospital for Mothers and Babies,
Woolwich, London

HM+M H M + M Publishers
AYLESBURY, ENGLAND

© Betty R. Sweet & Irene F. Cape 1976

First edition, published by
H M + M Publishers Ltd.
Milton Road, Aylesbury, Buckinghamshire, England

ISBN 0 85602 027 3

Acknowledgements

We should like to thank all those who have helped by giving their time, advice and encouragement, in particular Mr. C. K. Vartan, formerly Consultant Obstetrician to The British Hospital for Mothers and Babies, Woolwich, Miss H. M. M. McNie, Consultant Obstetrician, The British Hospital for Mothers and Babies, Woolwich, and Miss G. T. McCarthy, Consultant in Neuro-Paediatrics, Chailey Heritage and the Royal Alexandra Hospital for Children, Brighton, who read the scripts and gave helpful criticism on the anatomy and physiology, obstetrics and paediatrics respectively, also Mrs. J. Clark for contributing the Family Planning chapter, Miss I. G. Cooper for her help and hard work in producing the diagrams, and Miss S. West for help with the glossary. We are grateful to Mrs. M. Lewis, Mrs. P. Pitcher and Miss M. B. Wilde who typed the script. Finally we should like to thank Mrs K. Berry, editor of the series, for her help and advice, and the publishers for their patience and guidance throughout the production of this book.

Manufactured in Great Britain by
Hunt Barnard Printing Ltd,
Aylesbury, Buckinghamshire, England

Contents

Preface vi

1 Introduction 1
2 The Female Pelvis and Reproductive Organs 4
3 Development of the Placenta and Fetus 31
4 The Physiology and Diagnosis of Pregnancy 48
5 Ante-natal Care 56
6 Normal Labour: Physiology and Management 70
7 Normal Puerperium: Physiology and Management 91
8 The Newborn Baby 100
9 Neo-natal Complications: Low Birth-weight Babies 115
10 The Complications of Pregnancy 130
11 The Complications of Labour 147
12 The Complications of the Puerperium 163
13 Family Planning 168

Bibliography 177

Glossary 178

Index 183

Preface

This book is one of four written with the aim of providing guidance for student nurses undertaking the various options or modules of experience required in their general training. These four modules — obstetrics, geriatrics, psychiatry and community care — are not to be considered as separate entities but as complementary to one another and designed to provide an opportunity for student nurses to see their work in the broad human setting, including both the hospital and the community.

It is envisaged that this small book will give the student nurse a basic understanding of normal obstetric care and a brief introduction to some abnormal conditions which might affect mother and baby. Armed with this knowledge, it is hoped that nurses will find the care of mothers and babies an enjoyable and interesting experience. For those who wish to delve more deeply into this subject, there are suggestions for further reading at the end of the book, and a glossary of some obstetric terms and conditions.

The authors hope that this book will help the nurse to realize that, although expectant or nursing mothers are, in most instances, less physically dependent than many other patients, their needs are as great in that they require constant support, teaching and help as they adjust to the physical and emotional demands of pregnancy, labour and motherhood, and also to endeavour to see mothers and babies in the context of the family and the community in which they live.

Although this book has been written primarily for student nurses undertaking the obstetric option during their general training, it is hoped that it will also be of value to others involved in obstetric care. On the eventual implementation of the report of the Committee on Nursing (the Briggs' Report), this volume would provide a sound basic textbook for all learners taking the obstetric module.

Nursing and midwifery are considered 'caring professions', and we hope that this small volume will further the concept of care in this age of technology, as caring is still of prime importance in the practice of midwifery.

July 1976

BETTY R. SWEET
IRENE F. CAPE

1. Introduction

Although childbirth is an everyday occurrence, the moment of birth almost invariably produces rejoicing and a sense of achievement for both the mother and those attending her. Nowadays the husband is often present with his wife throughout labour and therefore shares with her the experience of childbirth and joy at the birth of their baby.

Today's mothers are carefully supervised by midwives and doctors during pregnancy, and can attend classes to prepare them for labour and motherhood. They have shorter labours than ever before, conducted by highly skilled personnel and, a few hours after delivery, are ambulant and making a rapid recovery. Yet despite these modern advances, mothers still value greatly the personal contact and care of kind, approachable staff who are able to meet their individual requirements with understanding and sympathy.

The great advances in obstetric care which have taken place in this century, together with medical and social improvements, have markedly reduced both maternal and fetal mortality and morbidity rates and hence, in England and Wales, childbirth is now safer than has ever been recorded. From the beginning of the century until 1935, the maternal mortality rate was very high, between four and five per thousand births, the commonest cause of death being puerperal sepsis. Over the last 40 years this rate has dropped dramatically to 0·12 per 1 000 total births in 1974 (including deaths due to abortion). Infant mortality rates have also fallen remarkably from 140 per 1 000 live births at the beginning of the century to 16·3 per 1 000 in 1974. The decline in mortality rates is attributed to a variety of reasons, both social and medical. Improved living standards, better nutrition and the education of the public have greatly benefited the health of the nation. Other major factors contributing to the fall in the death rate include: the advent of antenatal clinics (1919), the introduction of sulphonamides and antibiotics (1930s/1940s), advances in microbiology, improvements in anaesthetic, obstetric and surgical techniques, and increased use of oxytocic drugs and blood transfusion. Infant mortality rates have been further reduced by immunization against infectious diseases.

Mothers and babies today also benefit from well-trained midwives, obstetricians and paediatricians. Before the first Midwives Act of 1902 there was no national training or supervision of midwives, and, indeed, any woman could call herself a midwife, the word meaning 'with woman'. Since the implementation of the Act, midwives have been trained in schools approved by the Central Midwives Board and are now highly skilled practitioners of normal midwifery in their own right. At the end of the last century only a few doctors had any knowledge or experience of midwifery as it was considered improper for a man to attend a woman in labour, but now obstetrics is part of every medical student's curriculum and many doctors undergo further training for this very specialized branch of medicine. Midwives and doctors now work together, midwives referring any deviation from the normal to their medical colleagues.

In recent years neonatal paediatrics has developed into a specialty of its own and paediatricians are now involved in the care of the healthy newborn as well as those who are ill or immature. Many babies who, only a few years ago, would have died in the early neonatal period, now survive after intensive care in special care baby units.

The trend towards hospital confinement continues and today over 90 per cent of women in Britain have their babies in hospital. In an attempt to combine the safety of the hospital with the comforts of home and family life, however, and to free beds for more hospital deliveries, many mothers are transferred home within two or three days of delivery to be cared for by the community midwife and the family doctor. The community midwife will have assessed the patient's home during the antenatal period to ensure that it is suitable and that there is adequate help available for the care of the recently delivered mother and her young baby.

Emergency Obstetric Units (often called Maternity Flying Squads) are maintained throughout Britain to take obstetric personnel and equipment rapidly to the home (or small hospital) if urgent need arises in pregnancy, labour or the puerperium. Domino schemes are now gradually replacing home confinements whereby, instead of delivering a woman in her own home, the community midwife accompanies her to hospital in labour, and delivers her there. Then, if the general practitioner obstetrician is satisfied with the condition of both mother and baby, they are returned home by ambulance a few hours after delivery. The advantages of this scheme are that the patient is delivered in hospital where emergency facilities and consultant care are readily available should unexpected complications arise, yet she is only away from home for a few hours and has continuity of care from those she knows during the whole of her confinement. In addition, the fact that the community midwife and general practitioner obstetrician can take their patient into a consultant unit and care for her there is one further step on the road to a truly unified health service which was one of the main aims of reorganization in 1974.

With the exciting advances in ante-natal care, labour and neonatal paediatrics, and the move towards early transfer home in the puerperium, post-natal care has tended to recede into the background. However, the current social problems of child abuse and emotional deprivation accentuate the need for skilled care from the beginning of motherhood and in the early days of a new baby's life. This skilled care is available initially from the midwife, and later from the health visitor who visits the mother in her own home and meets her at the Child Health Clinic.

Family life has changed much over the years, children are now more often planned, families are smaller and may be isolated from other close relatives; thus the husband of today has a greater role to play in supporting his wife throughout her confinement and subsequently in the day-to-day upbringing of the children. Because many husbands require some preparation to equip them for their role, antenatal classes are now being held to meet the needs of both parents. More liberal visiting in maternity hospitals, especially by the mother's own children, and the planned early transfer schemes help to promote family life and minimize any disruption which may occur. Nurses undertaking the obstetric module should endeavour to understand the effect which the arrival of a new baby may have on all members of the family, and the adjustment each may have to make.

2. The Female Pelvis and Reproductive Organs

In order to gain maximum benefit from the following chapters and therefore to understand the concepts, physiological events, hazards, treatment and aspects of care in this introduction to obstetrics, some knowledge must first be acquired of the normal structure and related function of the female pelvis and reproductive organs.

Structure becomes relevant, and even fascinating, if it is remembered that throughout the human body it is related to function. The formation of not only each organ, but each *part* of each organ is directly related to the job it has to do. On this premise, any deviation from normal structure as a result of imperfect development, injury or disease will either constitute a hazard, or adversely affect function.

Knowledge of facts, however, is not enough. In order to reason and understand, students need some explanation of the facts; they need to know *how* and *why*. An attempt is made in this and successive chapters to explain briefly the relevant significance of stated facts.

The female pelvis

Throughout the reading of this section, the student is advised to examine a model pelvis to facilitate the identification of landmarks and the reasoning out of the text.

The bones of the pelvis

In contrast to the male pelvis built for activities requiring great strength, the essential features of a 'good' gynaecoid (female) pelvis are that its size and shape are adequate for the fetus to traverse during birth; its structure is therefore adapted to this end. The pelvis (or pelvic girdle) is a relatively light but very strong bony ring formed of four irregular bones:

2 innominate bones, 1 sacrum, 1 coccyx

The bones of the pelvis have some roughened surfaces for the attachment of strong skeletal muscles, and prominences, e g spines or tuberosities for the attachment of ligaments.

The *two innominate bones* one on either side of the sacrum, form all but the posterior part of the pelvis.

Each innominate bone is formed of three parts:
the ilium, the ischium, and the pubis
which begin to ossify separately in cartilage during development before birth. Their ossification is completed by twenty-five years of age, when the three bones have fused together to form one innominate bone, but the parts are still referred to.

The *ilium* forms the upper part of each innominate bone, the upper border of which is known as the iliac crest. The *two iliac crests* form the highest and widest parts of the pelvic girdle, are especially prominent in thin people, and can be felt in all but the obese. A marked ridge, the *ilio-pectineal line*, runs across the lower inner aspect of each ilium forward towards the pubis. The two lines, one on either side of the pelvic girdle, are of great obstetric significance as they form part of the *pelvic brim* (see Fig. 1).

The *ischium* forms the lowest part of each innominate bone. At the base of each is the large, solid *ischial tuberosity* which takes the weight of the body in the sitting position. These tuberosities also form the lateral walls of the true pelvis and therefore their positioning affects the diameter of the pelvic outlet. Of far greater obstetric significance, however, are the two *ischial spines*, small projections lying above and behind the ischial tuberosities, which, if they project inwards more than usual, significantly narrow the transverse diameter of the pelvic outlet. They are also used to assess the distance of the fetal head from the pelvic outlet during labour.

The *pubis* forms the front part of each innominate bone and of the pelvic girdle. The two bones meet anteriorly to form the most shallow part of the pelvis at the symphysis pubis, about 4 cm deep. Each pubic bone has a central body and two lateral arms or *rami*. The lower border of each body and inferior ramus on either side of the symphysis forms a *subpubic arch* of at least 90° in a good gynaecoid pelvis. The wider the arch the greater the ease with which the fetal head can escape from the confines of the pelvic cavity during labour.

The *sacrum*, a wedge-shaped bone consisting of five fused vertebrae forms the posterior part of the pelvic girdle and the lower end of the vertebral canal, with only the coccyx below it. The canal through which the human fetus has to pass at birth is curved, with the posterior concave wall formed by the sacrum being 12 cm, that is three times as deep as the anterior wall formed by the pubic bones (4 cm). This sacral curve makes the human pelvis a difficult one for the fetus to pass through, which difficulty both the uterus and the mother have to work extremely hard to overcome. The sacrum is also curved forwards slightly from side to side, forming a *sacral hollow* which allows room for the fetal head to lie comfortably in the pelvis once it has descended past the pelvic brim. Jutting forward over the top of the sacral hollow is the *sacral promontory*, the projecting upper border of the first sacral segment. The distance between the symphysis pubis and the sacral promontory is important because a reduced diameter could delay or prevent descent of the fetus. However, in all but about two per cent. of women in Britain the canal is adequate for the fetus to pass through safely.

The sacrum joins the two innominate bones forming a wedge between them. It gives attachment to ligaments and muscles, and passage to nerves and blood vessels through its four pairs of foramina.

The *coccyx*, composed of four fused vertebrae, is a small triangular structure about 3 cm long with the base uppermost, articulating with the lower end of the sacrum. It gives attachment to ligaments, to the strong levatores ani (deep muscles of the pelvic floor) and to muscle fibres of the anal sphincter.

The joints of the pelvis

The two innominate bones, the sacrum and the coccyx are joined in four places, each forming a cartilaginous (or slightly movable) joint:

> two *sacro-iliac joints* formed by the junction of the ilium with the first two sacral vertebrae on either side;
>
> the *sacro-coccygeal joint* at the junction of the sacrum with the coccyx below; and
>
> the *symphysis pubis* in front of the pelvic girdle, at the junction of the two pubic bones in the midline.

These joints are usually immobile in the non-pregnant state, but due to the hormonal action of one of the group of progesterones, slight softening and therefore mobility occurs in pregnancy which fractionally increases the pelvic measurements and may cause sacro-iliac strain, felt as back-ache, especially in a multiparous woman. The sacro-coccygeal joint allows the coccyx to move back out of the way during delivery.

The ligaments of the pelvis

Ligaments are cords of fibrous connective tissue binding one bone to another in order to add strength and stability to structures and joints. There are important pairs of ligaments attached to the pelvis:

> *Two pairs of wide sacro-iliac ligaments* from the sacrum to the ilium; one ligament over the front and one over the back of each sacro-iliac joint. The posterior ones are the strongest in the body, and are most important in maintaining a stable frame.
>
> There are also two other pairs of important ligaments:
>
> (i) the *sacro-tuberous ligaments* which pass from the lateral borders of the sacrum and coccyx to each ischial tuberosity;
>
> (ii) the *sacro-spinous ligaments* which pass from the lateral borders of the sacrum and coccyx to each ischial spine. They lie in front of the sacro-tuberous ligaments. Apart from helping to maintain the stability of the pelvis, they form the lateral and posterior parts of the pelvic outlet.

The areas of the pelvis

The bony pelvis is divided at the level of the pelvic brim into two parts: the *false pelvis* which lies above the pelvic brim and is of no obstetric significance; it is formed by the wings of the iliac bones; and the *true pelvis* below, which is very important in obstetrics.

The **true pelvis** is the curved bony canal through which the fetus must pass during birth. It consists of a *brim, cavity* and *outlet*. If any one diameter of the pelvis is abnormally short at any of these levels, cephalo-pelvic disproportion may occur; that is to say, the fetal head may be unable to pass through. It is important for the student to know the average dimensions of the pelvic brim, cavity and outlet of a gynaecoid pelvis, in order to understand the relationship between pelvic abnormality and the complications of labour.

1. The **brim of the pelvis** forms the upper limit of the true pelvis. In a normal female pelvis, it is approximately oval, with the sacral promontory jutting forward posteriorly. (It could be described as apple-shaped, with the indentation of the

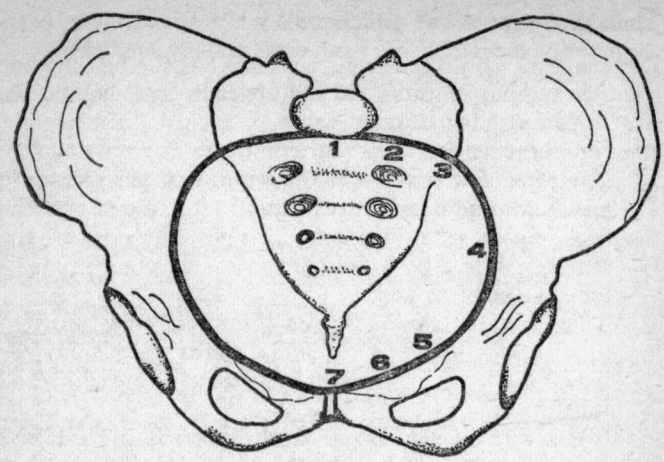

Fig. 1. The pelvic brim.

1 Sacral Promontory. 2 Sacral Wing. 3 Sacro-iliac Joint. 4 Ilio-pectineal Line.
5 Ilio-pectineal Eminence. 6 Superior Pubic Ramus. 7 Symphysis Pubis.

	ANTERO-POSTERIOR	OBLIQUE	TRANSVERSE
 BRIM	11·0 cm	12·0 cm	13·0 cm
 CAVITY	12·0 cm	12·0 cm	12·0 cm
 OUTLET	13·0 cm	12·0 cm	10·0 cm

Fig. 2. Average measurements of the pelvis.

stalk where the sacral promontory juts forward.) The pelvic brim forms the inlet to the birth canal and is bounded by:

the symphysis pubis and the upper, inner border of the superior pubic rami anteriorly,
the ilio-pectineal lines and eminences laterally, and
the sacro-iliac joints and the wings and promontory of the sacrum posteriorly (see Fig. 1).

The approximate measurements of the average gynaecoid pelvic brim. The *anterior-posterior diameter*, also known as the true conjugate, is measured from the centre of the promontory of the sacrum to the upper border of the symphysis pubis. However, the actual space available for the fetal head extends from the sacral promontory to the inside of the upper surface of the symphysis pubis and this, called the obstetrical conjugate,

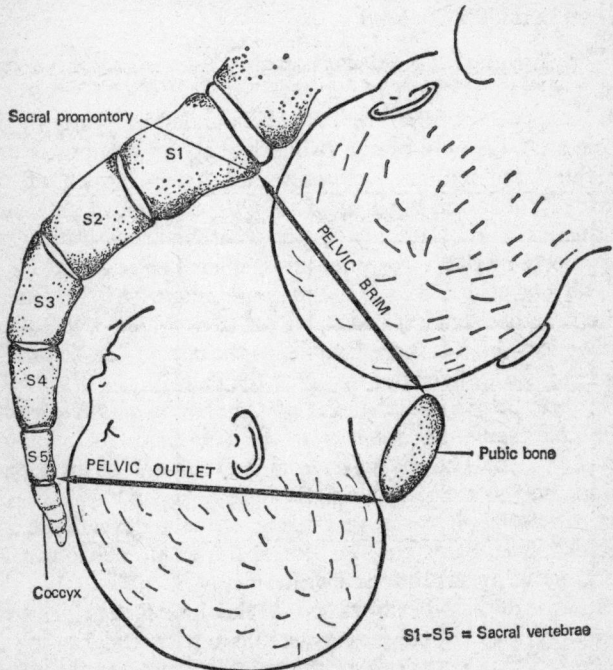

Fig. 3. The fetal head entering the pelvic brim and passing through the pelvic outlet.

measures 11 cm. It is the smallest diameter of the brim and therefore cannot afford to be reduced as, for example, by an excessive protrusion of the sacral promontory.

The *oblique diameters*, measured from the sacro-iliac joints to the opposite ilio-pectineal eminences, are 12 cm in length. The *transverse diameters*, measured from the points which are furthest apart, are 13 cm long.

2. The **cavity of the pelvis** lies between the pelvic brim above and the outlet below, being circular in shape. As the posterior wall of the cavity formed by the sacrum (12 cm) is concave, and three times deeper than the anterior wall at the symphysis pubis (4 cm), the descent of the fetus during labour follows a curved path.

The *measurements of the pelvic cavity*. The antero-posterior, oblique and transverse diameters are all equal, approximately 12 cm, at mid-cavity level.

3. The **outlet of the pelvis** is diamond-shaped and is sited at two levels.

The upper, the *obstetrical outlet* is bounded anteriorly by the pubic arch, laterally by the two ischial spines and posteriorly by the sacro-spinous ligaments and lower border of the sacrum. The lower, the *anatomical outlet* is bounded anteriorly by the pubic arch, laterally by the two ischial tuberosities, and posteriorly by the sacro-tuberous ligaments and coccyx.

The obstetrical outlet is the more important, because it contains the smallest diameter of the whole pelvis; the anatomical outlet is more flexible, as the coccyx can be pushed backwards during labour to widen the exit.

The approximate measurements of the obstetrical pelvic outlet. The *antero-posterior diameter* is the longest diameter of the outlet, 13 cm. The *oblique diameters* do not end at fixed bony points, and so are of little importance.

The *transverse diameter*, measuring 10 cm between the two ischial spines, being the smallest of the whole pelvic canal is therefore of great obstetric significance.

Because of the differing shapes of the three planes (or levels) of the pelvic canal, the fetus is unable to pass straight through it. To facilitate easy descent, the greatest diameter of the fetal head engages in the greatest diameter of the canal. It therefore enters the brim through the transverse diameter, but to avoid the narrow transverse of the outlet, has to rotate through 90° in order to emerge from the pelvis through the long antero-posterior diameter.

The pelvic floor

This important structure is a muscular sling across the pelvic outlet, forming a strong floor to the pelvis, and supporting the organs above it. *Three canals* pierce the pelvic floor: the *vagina* anteriorly with the *urethra* lying in front of it, and the *anal canal* posteriorly. The muscles of the floor are divided into two layers, *deep* and *superficial* (see Fig. 4).

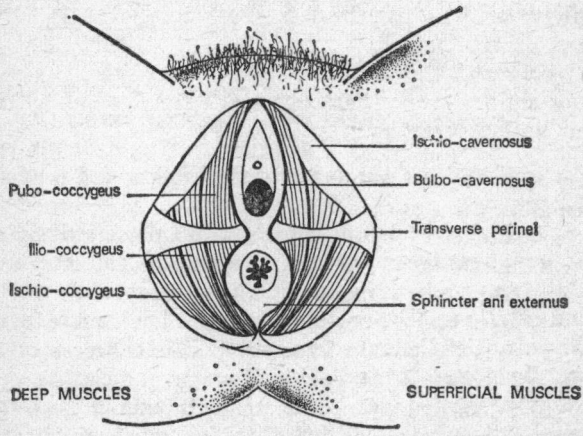

Fig. 4. The deep and superficial muscles of the pelvic floor.

The deep muscles (collectively known as the levatores ani) consist of a thick sheet of two powerful voluntary muscles sandwiched between pelvic fascia, which lie on either side of the midline. Each levator ani is divided into three parts, the ilio-coccygeus, the ischio-coccygeus and the pubo-coccygeus; these muscles are named after the parts of the innominate bones from which they arise in the front or sides of the bony pelvis, and the fibres pass backwards to be inserted into the coccyx and sacrum. In the midline, the fibres between the lower part of the vagina and the anal canal cross over to form part of the *perineal body*, while other fibres fuse with the walls of the canals passing obliquely through the floor. The pressure of the abdominal contents from above compresses the anterior wall of each oblique canal against its posterior wall, thus helping to maintain urinary and faecal continence. 'Levator ani' means 'lifter of the anus', and the contracted muscles keep the upper part of the anal canal pulled forwards at an angle to the rectum, only relaxing to allow defaecation to occur.

It is at the lowest level of the gutter-shaped levatores ani that the axis of the birth canal is angled, causing the fetus to take a turn forwards as it escapes from the pelvis, under the pubic arch.

The **superficial muscles** lie exterior to the deep layer. They consist of paired voluntary muscles on either side of midline, which do not form a continuous sheet, leaving gaps which are filled in by fascia. These muscles are:

(i) the bulbo-cavernosus (cavernosus is part of the clitoris)
(ii) the ischio-cavernosus; (iii) the transverse perineal.

Some of the muscles give additional strength to the pelvic floor, others form a loop around the urethra and vagina enforcing the effect of the deep muscle layer, while others form a strong sphincter (circular muscle with a purse-string action) around the anal canal. Normally in a state of contraction, these last can be relaxed voluntarily to allow defaecation to occur.

The perineal body, situated between the lower vagina and the anal canal, is composed of both deep *and* superficial muscles of the pelvic floor. Pyramidal in shape, with its apex deep, its base superficial and covered externally by skin, it is a buttress in the centre of the pelvic outlet. As the presenting part of the fetus descends during birth, the perineal body stretches and becomes wafer thin, often tearing unless an episiotomy (see p. 13) is performed to enlarge the vaginal outlet.

In addition to its aforementioned functions, the whole pelvic floor is involved in the second stage of labour, i e when the cervix is fully dilated. It undergoes enormous stretching and is displaced to allow the passage of the fetus through the birth canal.

Injury to the pelvic floor may be in the form of (*a*) perineal lacerations or (*b*) overstretching. (*a*) Perineal lacerations sometimes occur during the delivery of the baby and are classified as follows: a first degree tear involves only the fourchette (see vulva) and does not always require suturing; a second degree tear involves skin and muscle and will be sutured under a local anaesthetic; a third degree tear involves skin, muscle and rupture into the anal canal. It may lead to faecal incontinence and requires skilful suturing under general anaesthesia.

To avoid perineal laceration an episiotomy may be carried out; this is a surgical incision into the perineum to enlarge the vaginal orifice. The incision may be in the *midline* from the fourchette and directed towards the anus or, more commonly, *medio-lateral*, that is from the fourchette again but at about 30 to 40 degrees from the midline, the advantage of the latter being that, should it extend, it will not involve the anal sphincter. If required, an episiotomy is performed in the second stage of labour, when the perineum is distended by the presenting part, and is preceded by infiltration of the perineum with 7-10 ml of a local anaesthetic such as lignocaine 0·5% (50 mg).
(b) The healthy pelvic floor ignores slight changes in pressure due to the constant filling and emptying of the bladder and rectum. Even when the pregnant uterus increases its weight 15-20 times over a period of 40 weeks, the floor maintains its support. If, however, the floor becomes weakened for any reason, e g obstetric trauma such as overstretching of the muscle fibres, or severe obesity, this, coupled with an increase in the intra-abdominal pressure such as that caused by coughing, will cause a prolapse of the hitherto supported pelvic organs until the cause is treated and the weakness repaired.

The female genitalia

This term refers to those visible structures collectively known as the *external genitalia* or *vulva*; and the *internal genitalia*, consisting of the vagina, uterus, uterine (Fallopian) tubes and ovaries.

The external genitalia

These extend from the mons veneris (mound of Venus) anteriorly, to the perineal body posteriorly. The mons veneris and labia majora form the immediately visible part of the vulva; only when the labia are parted can the other structures be seen. The parts are very vascular, therefore any tears or incisions heal well.

The **mons veneris** is a rounded pad of fatty tissue and skin situated over the pubic bones; from puberty it is covered with hair which spreads along the labia majora below.

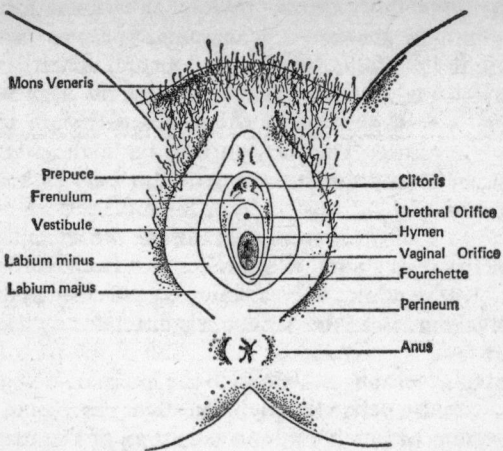

Fig. 5. Diagram of the external genitalia.

The **labia majora** are two thick folds of adipose tissue (fat) covered externally by skin, extending backwards from the mons veneris. They flatten out before merging with the perineal body posteriorly. On their outer surfaces they have hair, but the inner surfaces are smoother and have many sebaceous glands. The round ligaments from the uterus end in the anterior tissues of the labia majora, holding the fundus of the uterus forward to maintain its position of anteversion.

The **labia minora** are two thinner folds of smooth modified skin within the labia majora. They meet above the clitoris to form its hood-like *prepuce*, and below to form its frenulum, and then divide to enclose the *vestibule*, fusing together posteriorly at the *fourchette*. This last is commonly torn at the birth of the first baby.

The **clitoris** is a highly sensitive erectile structure about 2·5 cm long situated above and anterior to the urethral orifice, lying well-protected between the anterior folds of the labia. It contains tissue similar to that of the male penis, hollow and spongy, and in response to sexual stimulation becomes erect as it fills with blood.

The **vestibule** is the area enclosed by the labia minora, into which open:

the *urethra* anteriorly at its *meatus* about 2·5 cm below the clitoris; *Skene's ducts* open on either side of the meatus from corresponding sebaceous glands, and appear as two dimples which help to identify the urethral opening for the purpose of catheterization; and the *vagina* posteriorly at its *orifice* or *introitus*. This is covered by the *hymen*, a fold of skin which, in the virgin, is perforated to permit the menstrual flow, but is torn during sexual intercourse, and of which only tags remain after the birth of a baby. The openings of *Bartholin's glands* lie on either side of the vaginal orifice. They secrete mucus, which, together with the secretion from Skene's glands, pours forth in response to erection of the clitoris, acting as a lubricant for the vulva and vagina, thereby facilitating intercourse.

The vulva affords protection to the internal genitalia against physical injury and ascending infection. Its blood supply is mainly from two pairs of pudendal arteries. The nerve supply is to voluntary muscle and to glandular tissue. Occasionally, the vulva sustains lacerations during delivery and because it is a vascular structure it tends to bleed heavily but heals well.

The internal genitalia

The vagina

This is a muscular canal passing obliquely backwards from the vulva to the uterus. Its anterior and posterior walls are in contact with one another except at the top where the fornices surround the cervix, keeping them apart, and at the bottom where the vulval structures compress the *lateral* walls together.

The vagina is a passageway to the exterior for the menstrual flow and for the fetus during birth.

The uterus is set almost at right angles to the vagina, entering its upper third, hence the anterior vaginal wall (7·5 cm) is shorter than the posterior wall (10 cm). The upper end, or *vault* of the vagina forms a gutter round the *cervix* (lower end of the uterus) creating a large *posterior fornix*, a shallow *anterior fornix*, and two lateral *fornices*. The lower end of the vagina is partially closed by a hymen in the virgin (see above).

The wall of the vagina has four layers.

(*a*) An *inner lining* of modified skin (stratified squamous epithelium) thrown into folds or *rugae* which permit considerable distention during the birth of a baby. As with skin the surface layer of cells are being continuously shed. This lining is sensitive to the balance of oestrogens and progesterone in the blood, the state of which can be used for diagnostic and therapeutic purposes.

(b) A *layer of elastic connective tissue* plentifully supplied with small blood vessels, also thrown into folds.

(c) An *involuntary muscle layer* of inner circular and outer longitudinal fibres with some voluntary fibres around its exit.

(d) An *outer surrounding layer of connective tissue* carrying:
  branches of the vaginal arteries and veins;
  autonomic nerves from the sacral plexus to involuntary muscle tissue;
  branches of the pudendal nerves to voluntary muscle tissue; and
  lymphatic vessels draining lymph away to the inguinal, iliac and sacral nodes.

There are no glands in the vagina, but it is kept moist by alkaline secretions from the cervical glands, and serous exudate from its own numerous blood vessels. The vaginal fluid has an acid reaction with an average pH of 4·5 due to the presence of lactic acid formed by the action of *Doderlein's bacilli* (microorganisms which normally inhabit the vagina, i e *commensals*) on the glycogen in the epithelial lining cells. Normal vaginal acidity helps to prevent the growth of most organisms, but both before and after a woman's fertile years, the vagina is less acid and its resistance to infection thereby decreased.

The lower half of the *anterior* vaginal wall is related to the *urethra* and the upper half to the base of the *bladder*. A weakness of the wall will allow either of these structures to prolapse into it, causing a urethrocele or a cystocele affecting urinary continence.

The *posterior* vaginal wall is related to the *rectum* in its middle third, and this might prolapse into it causing a rectocele should the wall become weakened. The lower third of the posterior vaginal wall lies against the *perineal body*, and the upper third lies in front of the *pouch of Douglas* (see Fig. 6).

The uterus

This structure is a hollow, muscular organ, shaped like a flattened pear and situated in the middle of the true pelvis.

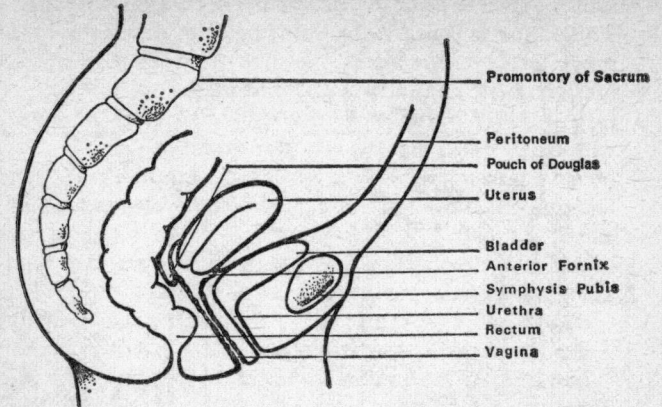

Fig. 6. Sagittal section through the female pelvis.

Its neck (the cervix) is inserted into the upper part of the vagina; its base (the fundus) is free, and in pregnancy rises up into the abdomen. The uterus is surprisingly small when not pregnant, about 7·5 cm long, 5 cm wide and 2·5 cm deep and weighs approximately 60 g. It is normally anteflexed and anteverted, i e bent and turned to the front of the pelvis.

The functions of the uterus are:

(1) to prepare for the reception of the fertilized ovum;
(2) to provide a suitable environment for the growth and development of the fetus, placenta and membranes throughout pregnancy; and
(3) to assist in their expulsion at term.

Structure. The uterus has two parts, the *body* and the *cervix* or neck (see Fig. 7).

1. The *body or corpus* is the upper two-thirds of the uterus, enclosing a triangular potential cavity in the non-pregnant state, continuous with the lumen of the uterine (Fallopian) tubes which are attached to its base at the two *cornua* (horns). The *fundus* is the dome-shaped part of the body above the level of the cornua. The body is the fast-growing part during pregnancy, the length of the uterus increasing to about 30 cm, its width to 23 cm, and its depth to 20 cm, and weighing about 1 000 g. The *isthmus* is the *narrow* short part (7 mm) at the junction of the body with the cervix below. It assumes im-

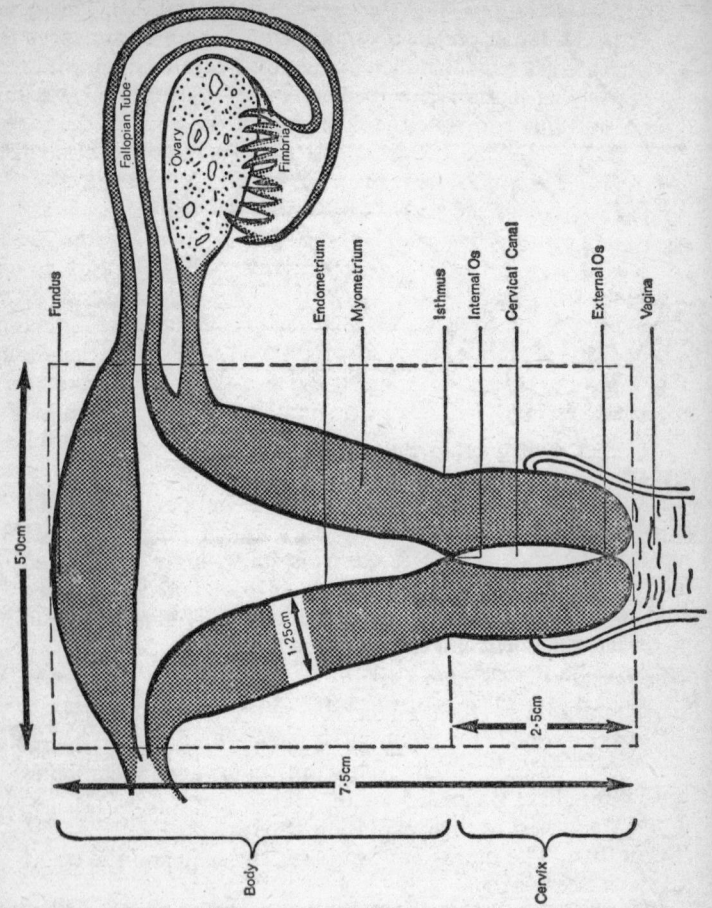

Fig. 7. The uterus, fallopian tube and ovary.

portance in pregnancy when it lengthens to some 25 mm by the tenth week, then grows rapidly until by the end of pregnancy it is nearly one quarter of the total length of the uterus and forms the *lower uterine segment*.

2. The *cervix or neck* is the cylindrical lower third of the non-pregnant uterus, and more than half its length projects downwards at a right-angle into the vagina. The *cavity* is a spindle-shaped canal; where it enters the uterus above is the *internal os*,

and where it opens into the vagina is the *external os*. The cervix grows wider in pregnancy, and before labour commences the upper fibres may be pulled up into the lower segment, shortening the canal. In labour the cervix is entirely effaced (see Fig. 20) and dilated, while the main part of the body of the uterus is actively forcing the fetus first against, and then through it. The *uterine wall* consists of:

(1) The *endometrium*, an *inner lining of mucous membrane*, is under constant hormonal control from puberty to the menopause. Its thickness and vascularity vary according to the stage and length of the menstrual cycle; the superficial layers of cells being shed periodically; the deep basal layer remaining and allowing regeneration to occur. The mucous membrane lining the cervix is known as the *endocervix*. It resembles the endometrium, but is thrown into deep folds known as the arbor vitae, tree of life, because its appearance resembles a trunk and branches. Deep glands produce *cervical mucus* which varies in viscosity at different times in the menstrual cycle. At the time of ovulation it is thin to assist the spermatozoa to reach their goal more easily; after a few days a thick plug is formed to protect the zygote (fertilized ovum) by keeping infection out of the uterus. If pregnancy does not occur the mucus is shed.

(2) The *myometrium* is a thick, strong, involuntary layer of muscle tissue forming seven-eighths of the thickness of the entire uterine wall with fibres running in various directions. During pregnancy the myometrium increases greatly in thickness, and the fibres become re-arranged in three layers; inner *circular* fibres in the lower part of the body and in the cervix and cornua; *interlacing* spiral fibres forming a middle layer which is thickest in the upper two-thirds of the body where the placenta is normally situated, because this arrangement has the special ability to constrict the bloodvessels which would otherwise bleed when the placenta separates; and *longitudinal* fibres forming strands which are the active expulsive force in labour and constitute the outer layer of the myometrium. The muscle-fibre arrangement around the cervix enables it to dilate in labour.

(3) The *perimetrium* is a layer of peritoneum covering the surface of the uterus except for a narrow area each side below the uterine (Fallopian) tubes. The perimetrium passes down

behind the uterus to cover the upper third of the posterior wall of the vagina and is then reflected back to form the *pouch of Douglas* before being attached to the anterior surface of the rectum. It only covers the front of the uterus as far down as the isthmus, and is then reflected up to pass over the top of the bladder, leaving the front of the cervix uncovered. All the pelvic organs and muscles that are not covered by peritoneum are covered by a sheet of pelvic fascia.

The vessels of the uterus. Two uterine and two ovarian arteries anastomose to provide the uterus with a rich blood supply. The uterine arteries are heavily coiled so that they can straighten as the uterus grows during pregnancy. Corresponding veins carry away the deoxygenated blood. Lymphatics drain via groups of nodes adjacent to the internal iliac blood vessels.

The uterine (or Fallopian) tubes

These are two patent, muscular tubes about 10 cm long, one on either side of the uterus, extending from the cornu laterally to the side wall of the pelvis where it curves downwards and backwards, ending in close proximity to the ovary. Each tube communicates at one end with the uterine cavity and at the other with the peritoneal cavity.

The layer of peritoneum which covers the uterus hangs like a sheet draped over its two outstretched arms (the uterine tubes), forming a double layer below them which is known as the *broad ligament*. The two layers are packed with pelvic fascia supporting the ovarian vessels and nerves which run between them. Each tube is described in 4 parts (see Fig. 7):

(*a*) *The interstitial part* is the opening into the tube through the uterine wall. It is about 1·25 cm long and is the narrowest part (1 mm).

(*b*) *The isthmus* is slightly less narrow, about 2·5 cm long, and distal to the cornu.

(*c*) *The ampulla* is a widened-out portion extending laterally for about 5 cm where fertilization takes place.

(*d*) The *infundibulum* is the trumpet-shaped lateral end of the tube, with its circumference fringed into finger-like processes called *fimbriae*. The longest of these is in contact with the ovary and is known as the fimbria ovarica. From the isthmus onwards there is no obvious lumen because of the maze of folds in the lining of the tube. At the end of the ampulla the tube opens into the peritoneal cavity.

The walls of the tubes have:

(1) *An inner lining of mucous membrane* continuous with the uterus. Many of the cells are ciliated to propel the ovum towards the uterus, and other non-ciliated ones secrete mucus, being known as goblet cells. This lining is packed into the longitudinal folds and pleats.

(2) A layer of *vascular connective tissue* outside the mucous layer.

(3) An *involuntary muscle layer* consisting of inner circular and outer longitudinal fibres to facilitate the passage of the ovum along the tube.

(4) An *outer peritoneal coat*, except on the inferior border, which becomes continuous with the broad ligament.

Functions

1. The uterine tubes allow spermatozoa to pass from the uterine cavity to the ampulla.

2. From puberty to the menopause they receive the ejected ovum from the ovary following ovulation, and provide a suitable environment for fertilization to occur (usually in the ampulla). The tubes propel the ovum to the uterine cavity where *either* it embeds if fertilized,

or it is discharged in the menstrual flow.

The fertilized ovum takes 5 or 6 days to reach the uterine cavity, slowed down by the convolutions in the lining of the tube; if these were absent the ovum would reach the uterus before the endometrium was thick enough to sustain it or the fertilized ovum had developed the villi essential for embedding.

The ovaries

These two almond-shaped organs vary considerably in structure and function, according to age, parity and the stage of the menstrual cycle. They are situated inside the peritoneal cavity slightly posterior to the uterine tubes, lying in depressions on the lateral pelvic walls, known as the *ovarian fossae*.

During the child-bearing years the ovaries measure approximately 3 cm long, 2 cm wide and 1 cm thick, but later in life they atrophy (see Fig. 7). The ovaries are attached to the posterior layer of the broad ligament by a narrow fold named the *mesovarium*, which carries the blood vessels and nerves to and from the gonads. On its medial aspect each ovary is attached to the cornu of the uterus by the *ovarian ligament*, which runs within the broad ligament, at the back of the uterus. The lateral pole of the ovary is attached to one of the fimbria of the tube, and also to the pelvic wall. Despite all these supports the ovaries do not return to their original niche once they have been lifted out of the pelvis by a pregnancy.

The structure of the ovaries

Each ovary consists of an *inner medulla* and an *outer cortex* which is covered by a layer of specialized tissue, the *germinal epithelium*.

(1) The **medulla** consists of connective tissue, some involuntary muscle and many large blood vessels, lymphatics and nerves. It supports and nourishes the cortex.

(2) **The cortex** consists of stroma of a much denser texture than the medulla. It is in this toughest part of the ovary that the ovarian (Graafian) follicles and corpora lutea develop. The outer layer of the cortex, the germinal epithelium, is continuous with the peritoneum of the broad ligament, and is formed of a layer of cubical cells. The surface of the ovary after puberty is wrinkled and grey, in contrast to the smooth, shiny peritoneum, due to the eruption of numerous Graafian follicles through the germinal epithelium.

The functions of the ovaries

There are two related functions of the ovaries:

(1) *to produce ova* (egg-cells) for fertilization, and during this process,

(2) *to produce hormones* which will aid female development, and help to maintain pregnancy, should it occur, during the first three months. Incidental to these two functions is the menstrual (monthly) cycle, the preparation of the endometrium for a possible pregnancy, and its subsequent shedding when pregnancy fails to occur.

1. *The production of ova*

It is estimated that the two ovaries between them harbour up to 300 000 primordial follicles in their cortices, most of which never reach full maturity. Development of these follicles depends on stimulation by a gonadotrophic (sex-gland-stimulating) hormone from the anterior lobe of the pituitary gland, known as the *follicle stimulating hormone* (FSH), which usually begins at about the age of ten years (the onset of puberty), when groups of cells become cystic and form the Graafian or ovarian follicles. These contain fluid (liquor folliculi) which increases the size of the cystic follicles. Within each follicle, and lining it, specialized cells develop which surround and nourish the ovum, and produce *oestrogen*. As the Graafian follicles develop they rise towards the surface of the ovary, appearing as a bulge under its surface. Only one of this group, rarely two or more, is likely to achieve ovulation each month, from alternate ovaries, fourteen days before the next menstrual period is due to commence; this involves rupturing through the outer layers of cortex.

So far, the events taking place in the ovary have been due to the influence of FSH, one of the gonadotrophic hormones. Subsequent events are due to the influence of a second gonadotrophin, the *luteinizing hormone* (LH), also produced by the anterior lobe of the pituitary gland, which now causes the Graafian follicle, protruding from the surface of the ovary, to rupture, and the egg (ovum) to be released (*ovulation*). The ovum floats out, normally to be attracted into the trumpet-like end of the uterine tube. Fertilization, should it occur, usually takes place in the outer third of the tube within 24 hours of ovulation.

The remaining cells of the Graafian follicle proliferate and become lutein cells, which, with the blood that escapes at the site of rupture, produces the yellow pigment in the mass of cells which is now called the *corpus luteum*. This continues to produce oestrogen, but in addition secretes *progesterone*, the hormone to thicken the endometrium ready for the ovum to embed. If pregnancy occurs, the corpus luteum continues to produce oestrogen and progesterone until the 12th week of pregnancy. If the ovum is not fertilized, and so dies within a day or two, the corpus luteum shrinks and ceases to secrete. It eventually forms a small white pit or scar, called the corpus albicans. During the 30 or more years known as a woman's 'fertile period' (from age 15 to 45 years) the ovaries may produce some 350 fully ripened ova, of which only two or three, on average, are likely to be fertilized and then develop into new individuals.

The opportunity for fertilization to occur can be inhibited by birth control methods, or enhanced by the use of fertility drugs which stimulate ovulation in women who fail to conceive.

2. *The production of hormones*

The ovaries are endocrine glands, in that they secrete two hormones, *oestrogen* and *progesterone*. The secretion of both these hormones is controlled by the two gonadotrophic hormones from the anterior lobe of the pituitary gland:

(1) the **follicle stimulating hormone** (FSH) concerned with:

(*a*) conversion of primordial follicles into Graafian follicles;

(*b*) production of **oestrogen** by the Graafian follicles; and

(*c*) maturation (ripening) of the ova.

(2) the **luteinizing hormone** (LH) concerned with:

(*a*) ovulation, development of the corpus luteum, and

(*b*) production of **progesterone** by the corpus luteum.

Like all trophic hormones, the production of the pituitary gonadotrophins is determined by the level of the hormone which they control in the bloodstream. In the case of oestrogen production, when the level of oestrogen is low in the blood, the FSH is stimulated to trigger-off the production of more oestrogen, until the rising level of oestrogen in the blood inhibits further production of FSH. As the oestrogen level falls, the feedback mechanism recommences.

Progesterone secretion is controlled in exactly the same way.

Oestrogens. This is the name given to a group of about 20 similar hormones, secreted mainly by the Graafian follicles within the ovary, although smaller amounts are produced by the corpora lutea and the adrenal cortex. They pass to the liver after use, to be converted into a form suitable for excretion in the urine. During pregnancy, oestriol is produced by the fetal adrenals and liver, and by the placenta, and excreted in the mother's urine; thus the levels can be measured in a series of 24-hour urine specimens, to assess fetal health.

Functions of the oestrogens. (1) At puberty they are responsible for the following changes:

(*a*) growth and development of the uterus, tubes and vagina;
  (*b*) characteristic female deposits of fat over the breasts and hips, giving shape to the body; the growth of axillary and pubic hair; and
  (*c*) onset of the menstrual cycle.

(2) They help to control the phases of the menstrual cycle, according to their changing levels in the bloodstream, and are thought to cause pre-menstrual salt and water retention.

(3) At ovulation, oestrogens stimulate the cervical glands to produce more and thinner mucus so that:
  (*a*) the alkaline mucus protects the spermatozoa from the acidity of the vaginal secretions; and
  (*b*) the cervix is more readily traversed by the spermatozoa.

(4) During pregnancy oestrogens
  (*a*) cause proliferation of the lining of the vagina, and increase its production of glycogen, which, when acted upon by Doderlein's bacilli, produces lactic acid to protect the vagina and uterus from infection;
  (*b*) cause the uterine muscle to grow;
  (*c*) suppress ovulation;
  (*d*) inhibit lactation until the birth of the child; and
  (*e*) cause water and electrolyte retention in body tissues.

Progesterone

This hormone is secreted only by:
  (*a*) the corpus luteum until it atrophies (therefore only after ovulation has occurred) for up to ten days in the hope that fertilization of the ovum may occur; and
  (*b*) the placenta from the 12th week of pregnancy until the time of delivery.

If pregnancy occurs, the corpus luteum remains active, producing progesterone for about three months until the placenta takes over this function—then it atrophies. After use, progesterone is converted by the liver to pregnanediol, in which form it is excreted in the urine.

The functions of progesterone. (1) It is responsible:
  (*a*) for the secretory phase of the menstrual cycle. To this end it causes proliferation of the endometrium, to form a thick tissue with deep glands and blood vessels; a bed prepared to create a suitable environment that will encourage the fertilized ovum to embed and pregnancy to develop; and

(b) with oestrogen, for the retention of salt and water in the pre-menstrual (regressive) phase of the cycle.
(2) It prepares, and maintains, the decidua in pregnancy.
(3) It is concerned with development of the glandular breast tissue in early pregnancy in readiness for lactation.
(4) It relaxes plain muscle throughout the body, but particularly in the uterus, thereby inhibiting the onset of labour until the level of progesterone falls in the bloodstream at term, possibly due to ageing of the placenta.

The menstrual cycle

The menstrual cycle is the process by which the endometrium lining the body of the uterus proliferates in preparation for the reception of the fertilized ovum, and in the absence of fertilization is shed. This process is continuous in women from the ménarche to the menopause, usually being interrupted only when pregnancy occurs. The menstrual cycle is controlled by *ovarian hormones* which are secreted under the influence of the *gonadotrophic hormones* from the *anterior lobe of the pituitary gland* (see pp. 23–26). This gland, in its turn, is controlled by the *hypothalamus* (an adjacent nerve centre) which can be affected by the emotional state of the woman, and give rise to amenorrhoea in conditions of stress.

The endometrial phases of the menstrual cycle.

The menstrual cycle is described as lasting 28 days from the first day of one menstrual period to the first day of the next. In fact many women do not menstruate at regular 28-day intervals, unless taking oral contraceptives, which cause an artificial regularity. Although cycle-length may vary, the time between ovulation and menstruation is constant at 14 days.
(1) **The menstrual phase.** As the first day of the menstrual flow is usually called Day 1, this phase will be considered first. If the ovum is not fertilized, the corpus luteum begins to degenerate towards the end of the previous cycle and its output of oestrogens and progesterone falls. The endometrium, dependent on these hormone levels, disintegrates, and, apart from the basal layer, is expelled, accompanied by bleeding from the many blood vessels which had caused its high vas-

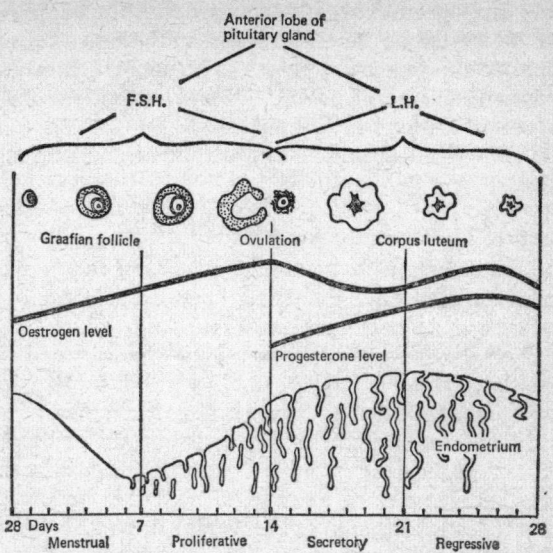

Fig. 8. Diagram of the menstrual cycle.

cularity. The amount of blood loss varies between 60 and 180 ml, the normal length of menstruation being from 3 to 6 days.

(2) **The proliferative phase.** Following menstruation, the growth of a Graafian follicle in one ovary means that the level of circulating oestrogens will rise again, and under this influence, after a brief resting period, the endometrium will begin to proliferate. Most of the endometrial growth takes place during this phase, but the glands remain narrow and straight. This phase is of variable length, but if the cycle is 28 days, lasts for 7–10 days.

(3) **The secretory phase.** Ovulation takes place at the end of the proliferative phase, and the corpus luteum is formed and secretes progesterone, which causes some further growth in the endometrium, but it is the glands which show the main change, becoming longer, dilated and tortuous. This phase lasts for about a week.

(4) **The regressive phase.** In the final week of the menstrual cycle, the congestion and vascularity of the endometrium increases still further; the glands become deeper and more

spiral in shape, and begin to collapse with the fall in oestrogen and progesterone levels. (Some authorities consider the secretory and regressive phases to be one which extends from ovulation to menstruation.) Water retention may cause discomfort during this last phase.

The cycle then recommences with the onset of menstruation.

The breasts

The female breasts, or mammary glands, are two hemispherical organs situated on the anterior chest wall. They develop in the fascia of the pectoralis major muscles to which they remain attached. Each breast covers an area which extends in depth from the 2nd to the 6th rib, and in width from the sternum to the mid-axillary line. The base is almost circular, except in its upper, outer aspect where it extends into the axilla. This part is known as the axillary tail of Spence. The apex of each breast has a circular area of loose pigmented skin about 2.5 cm in diameter called the *areola*. This is pink or pinkish-brown in the nullipara, but also varies according to the general colouring of

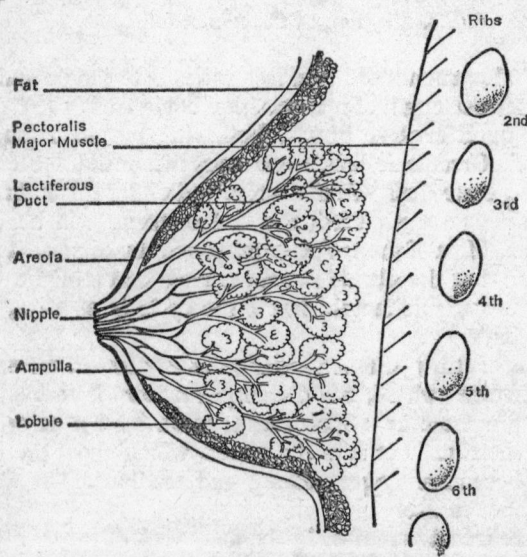

Fig. 9. A section through the breast.

skin and hair, and is darker in the parous woman. In the centre of the areola is the *nipple*, a small, highly sensitive, cylindrical structure, at about the level of the 4th intercostal space in the nullipara.

The size of the breast varies according to age, parity and individual build.

The function of the breasts is to produce milk for the baby.

The structure of the breasts

The breasts are composed largely of glandular tissue, surrounded by fat. Each breast consists of 15–20 *lobes*, which are separated from each other by fibrous tissue. The lobes are subdivided into *lobules*, each composed of numerous *alveoli*, which are the active secretory units and are connected by *ducts*. Milk secreted in the alveoli drains into these ducts which connect to form *lactiferous (milk carrying) tubules*. These widen out beneath the areola to form reservoirs for the milk called *ampullae*, and then become narrow again before opening on to the surface of the nipple (see Fig. 9).

The alveoli are lined with cubical epithelium which secretes milk and are surrounded by a layer of myo-epithelial cells which contract and expel the milk into the ducts. Around the lactiferous tubules near the nipple are smooth muscle fibres permitting a sphincter-like action.

The nipples are composed of erectile tissue and smooth muscle fibres covered by pigmented epithelium which has a wrinkled surface and is perforated by the minute orifices of the lactiferous tubules. Several small sebaceous glands open onto the surface of the areola around the nipple. The breasts are supplied with arterial blood from the internal and external mammary and the upper intercostal arteries, ready for their period of activity and development during pregnancy, in preparation for their ultimate function after the birth of the baby. The venous return of blood drains into the mammary and axillary veins.

Lymphatic vessels beneath the areola and between the lobes of the breasts drain freely into numerous axillary and mediastinal glands. There is also communication between the lymphatics of the two breasts.

Branches of the 4th, 5th and 6th thoracic cutaneous nerves

supply the breasts, conveying sympathetic fibres to involuntary muscle in the walls, the arterial blood vessels, the alveoli and lactiferous tubules. The breasts, however, are essentially under hormonal rather than nervous control.

The physiology of lactation

Lactation is inhibited in pregnancy by high levels of circulating oestrogen, which fall fairly rapidly after the end of labour, so allowing prolactin, which is released from the anterior lobe of the pituitary gland to become the dominating influence by about the third post-partum day. Before the milk 'comes in', the small amount of fluid secreted in the breasts is known as colostrum. The blood supply to the breasts increases considerably during pregnancy and remains high throughout lactation. This is essential for the production of an adequate supply of milk.

Under the influence of prolactin, tiny globules of milk form within the cells of the alveoli, and pass through the cell membrane into the ducts. Oxytocin from the posterior lobe of the pituitary gland causes contraction of the myo-epithelial cells around the ducts, so causing the secreted milk to pass into the lactiferous tubules. This sequence of events occurs physiologically following labour, but lactation is sustained by the stimulus of the baby sucking at the breast. In the absence of this stimulus, lactation will cease.

As the baby sucks, sensory stimuli cause oxytocin to be released, so permitting the 'letting-down' of the milk, or the 'draught reflex' as this conditioned reflex is called. The oxytocin also stimulates the further production of prolactin which promotes the secretion of more milk for the next feed.

3. Development of the Placenta and Fetus

Fertilization

The ovum, like all other human body cells, contains 46 chromosomes. Before an ovum is released monthly from alternate ovaries, it undergoes ripening changes, called maturation, during which an initial, unique reduction division (cell meiosis) results in 23 chromosomes being discarded. This leaves the ovum ready for an invasion of 23 chromosomes carried by the spermatozoon, which has also undergone a reduction division. The male seed comprises a head which contains the nucleus (with 23 chromosomes), a middle portion, and a tail which is very motile, enabling the spermatozoon to propel itself along the female genital tract.

During sexual intercourse some 300 000 000 spermatozoa may be deposited in the upper vagina, though eventually only one will achieve fertilization. Many do not survive the acidity of the vagina, others fail to negotiate the cervical canal and only the strongest survive the journey through the uterine cavity to the appropriate Fallopian tube. The ovum, which measures 0·15 mm in diameter and can just be seen by the naked eye, is much larger than the spermatozoon which is only 0·05 mm in length.

If, within two to three days of ovulation, spermatozoa reach the ovum in the Fallopian tube, fertilization is likely to take place. Several spermatozoa may penetrate the ovum, but only one fuses with its nucleus to effect fertilization. Once this has occurred, the now fertilized ovum secretes a substance which prevents further penetration by other spermatozoa.

Changes within the fertilized ovum, now known as the zygote, occur, and the 46 chromosomes form 22 pairs of autosomes and one pair of sex chromosomes. The zygote derives 22 autosomes and an x chromosome from the ovum and 22 autosomes and an x or a y chromosome from the spermatozoon, resulting in the pair of sex chromosomes being xx (female) or xy (male). Thus it is the sex chromosomes from the father which determines whether the baby will be a girl or a boy. Other characteristics are derived from both parents.

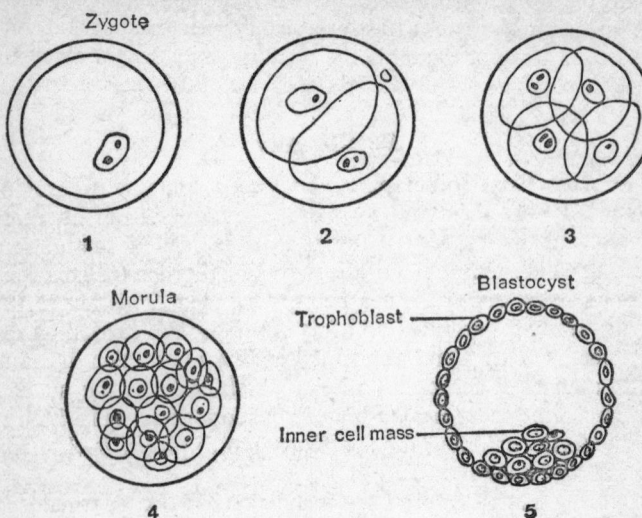

Fig. 10. Diagram to show the progression from a zygote to a blastocyst.

Segmentation and embedding of the ovum

After fertilization the zygote divides and subdivides as it travels along the Fallopian tube to the uterus. Within three or four days it has become a cluster of cells resembling a mulberry no larger than the ovum and is known as the morula. A small, cystic cavity develops in the morula after the structure, now known as the blastocyst, has entered the uterine cavity, 4 to 5 days after fertilization and 5 to 6 days after ovulation, coming to rest on the lining of the uterus. Inside the blastocyst is the inner cell mass from which the fetus develops. The outer layer of the blastocyst is then called the trophoblast which draws nourishment from the lining of the uterus as embedding occurs. (Later the trophoblast forms the placenta, which continues this function.) The trophoblastic cells secrete an enzyme which digests the endometrial cells, causing a small indentation into which the blastocyst sinks. This process continues until the whole blastocyst is embedded in the decidua (previously called the endometrium) and the site of entry then heals over. Implantation is usually complete within 10 days of fertilization. Slight bleeding sometimes occurs when the ovum embeds and the woman may mistake this for a scanty menstrual period. As the ovum grows it distends the decidua, and, by the twelfth week of pregnancy, fills the whole cavity of the uterus.

Formation of the decidua

While implantation of the ovum is taking place, thickening of the decidua continues. The corpus luteum does not degenerate 14 days after ovulation, as always occurs when the ovum remains unfertilized, but continues to grow and develop for three months under the influence of the hormone chorionic gonadotrophin, which is produced by the cells of the trophoblast. The production of the ovarian hormones, progesterone and oestrogen, therefore continues, progesterone being responsible for building up the decidua into a thick, vascular bed suitable for the implantation and nourishment of the ovum. (For other functions of progesterone and oestrogens, see pp. 25–26.)

Development of the placenta and embryo

During implantation, changes are not only taking place in the decidua, but also in the trophoblast and the inner cell mass. The trophoblast develops and will eventually form the placenta and chorion; the inner cell mass will form the embryo, cord and amnion.

Placental development

The cells of the trophoblast proliferate and differentiate into three layers:

(1) *syncitiotrophoblast* (also known as the syncitium), an outer mass of nucleated protoplasm without cell walls, which facilitates the absorption of substances from the surrounding circulating blood and also secretes the hormones of pregnancy;

(2) *cytotrophoblast* (or Langhan's layer), the middle layer of cells which have a selective action; and

(3) *mesoderm*, the inner, loose connective tissue layer which will later contain the fetal blood vessels. The mesoderm is continuous with the inner cell mass, the part where they meet being known as the body stalk.

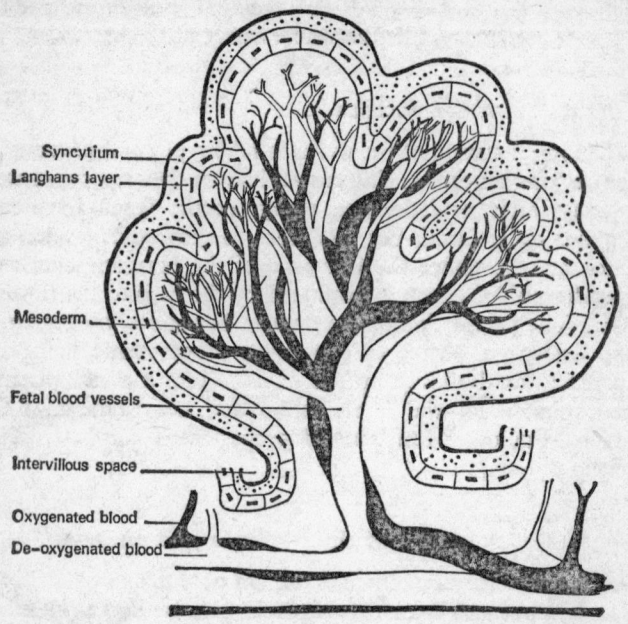

Fig. 11. Diagram of a chorionic villus (greatly enlarged).

Small projections, known as chorionic villi, develop all over the surface of the trophoblast and are composed of the three layers of cells mentioned above. These villi erode the maternal blood vessels and are thus bathed in pools of maternal blood from which they obtain their nourishment. The areas surrounding the villi which are filled with maternal blood are known as the inter-villous spaces.

Gradually the villi begin to branch, until they are intricate, tree-like structures, all composed of the three layers of cells described above. The longer villi are more deeply embedded in the decidua and are known as the anchoring villi, whereas the others float freely in the maternal blood spaces and are called the nutritive villi.

Fetal blood vessels form within the villi and unite to form larger vessels which pass through the body stalk to the inner cell mass. Food and oxygen pass from the maternal blood across the walls of the villi into the fetal blood and thence through the body stalk to the developing embryo. It should thus be understood that, under normal circumstances, fetal and maternal blood do not mix, because fetal blood is contained within its own vessels and separated from maternal blood by the walls of the villi.

During the third month of pregnancy the chorionic villi which lie deepest in the decidua continue to proliferate in an intricate manner to form the chorion frondosum which develops into the placenta. The remaining villi surrounding the blastocyst degenerate, leaving the chorion laeve (bald membrane) which becomes the membrane called the chorion.

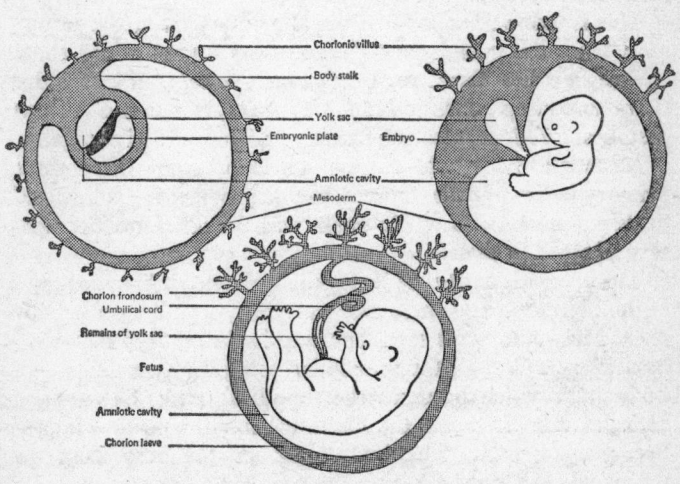

Fig. 12. Stages in embryonic development.

Embryonic development

Whilst the trophoblast is developing into the placenta, changes are occurring in the inner cell mass as the embryo is formed. Two small cavities appear:

(*a*) the *amniotic cavity* which is filled with fluid and lined with ectodermal cells; and

(*b*) the *yolk sac* which is lined with endodermal cells.

Mesodermal cells separate the two cavities. The area between the two cavities where the ectodermal, mesodermal and endodermal cells meet is known as the embryonic plate and it is from these three primary layers of cells that the embryo is formed between the third and eighth week of pregnancy. It is most important to realise that the developing fetus can be damaged by harmful substances, such as drugs or virus infections (e g rubella), at this very vulnerable stage of development, any resultant abnormality affecting the particular structures forming at that time.

The *ectodermal* cells form the nervous system, many epithelial structures including the skin, hair and nails, many endocrine (ductless) and exocrine (ducted) glands (they also form the amnion).

The *endodermal* cells form the alimentary tract, the respiratory tract and gonads, and the accessory organs of digestion.

The *mesoderm* forms the heart, blood vessels, all connective tissue including bones and blood, muscles, serous and mucous membrane linings, also the urinary and reproductive organs.

Although the whole embryo develops from these three primary layers of cells, more than one group may be involved in development of a whole organ with its differentiation into several types of tissue.

The amniotic cavity gradually enlarges until it fills the whole of the blastocyst and surrounds the embryo, yolk sac and body stalk. Most of the yolk sac is enclosed in the embryo and forms its alimentary canal, the remainder being incorporated in the body stalk which becomes the umbilical cord. The amnion enlarges until it meets the chorionic membrane to which it becomes adherent. The body stalk lengthens to form the umbilical cord, thus allowing the fetus freedom of movement in the liquor amnii (see p 40, fluid secreted by the amnion).

As early as the fourth week the fetal heart is formed and a rudimentary fetal circulation is developing. The fetal bones begin to ossify in about the fifth week. By the eighth week of pregnancy the embryo has a recognizable head, trunk and limbs and is now called a fetus. Growth and development of the fetus then continue throughout pregnancy.

The placenta, membranes and cord at term

The **placenta** is a round, flat organ which is attached to the decidua and normally situated in the upper segment of the uterus. Early in pregnancy it is larger than the fetus, but at term, because many of the fetal organs have taken over their own functions, it weighs approximately one sixth of the weight of the baby, i e 500–600 g. It is about 20 cm in diameter and 2·5 cm thick.

The placenta has two surfaces, fetal and maternal.

(a) The *fetal* surface is smooth and shiny, because it is covered with amnion, and bluish-mauve in colour. The umbilical cord enters the fetal surface, usually near the centre. The two umbilical arteries branch and radiate from the cord across this surface dividing into smaller branches, each supplying a cotyledon (see below), further dividing into capillaries in the villi. The network reforms as venous branches which traverse the fetal surface to form finally one umbilical vein in the cord.

(b) The *maternal* surface is attached to the decidua and is rougher and redder in colour than the fetal surface. It is composed of masses of chorionic villi which are arranged into about 20 lobes called cotyledons. Between the cotyledons are furrows called sulci, which are filled with little walls (septa) of decidua. The maternal surface may feel gritty to touch because of fibrin deposits which become calcified.

Functions of the placenta

The placenta does the work of a number of fetal organs which do not function, or fully function, during intra-uterine life, i e the lungs, the alimentary tract, the liver, the kidneys and certain endocrine glands.

(a) **Respiratory.** The fetus obtains its oxygen and excretes carbon dioxide via the placenta. Oxygen in the maternal blood in the intervillous spaces diffuses through the walls of the villi into the fetal blood and carbon dioxide from the fetal blood passes into the maternal circulation.

(b) **Nutritive.** The fetus obtains its food by the passage of absorbed nutritive substances from the mother's blood across the placenta; thus, in order to maintain her own health and nourish her unborn child, the mother must have a good diet in pregnancy.

The placenta selects the necessary digested foodstuffs which are circulating in the mother's blood in simple form: amino acids (proteins); monosaccharides, e g glucose (carbohydrates); fatty acids (fats), water and fat soluble vitamins and mineral substances. Some of these pass in solution directly across to the fetus by simple diffusion, whilst others are broken down into even simpler substances of low molecular weight by enzymes in the placenta before being suitable for fetal absorption.

(c) **Glycogenic.** The placenta stores glycogen which it can reconvert into glucose for the fetus, as required. During the later weeks of pregnancy the fetal liver takes over this function.

(d) **Excretory.** Waste products of metabolism diffuse across the placenta to the maternal blood, and are then excreted by the mother in addition to her own waste products.

(e) **Endocrinal.** The placenta produces several hormones, the main ones being:

(i) human chorionic gonadotrophin which is produced from the trophoblast in early pregnancy to maintain the corpus luteum, thereby ensuring an adequate supply of oestrogens and progesterone until the placenta is formed at about the 12th week. Chorionic gonadotrophin is excreted in the maternal urine and serves as the basis of diagnosis in pregnancy tests (see p. 55). The amount does not increase after the 14th week.

(ii) oestrogens and progesterone are produced by the placenta from about the 12th week, the amounts produced increasing as pregnancy advances (see pp. 25-26 for functions). The fetal adrenals are also concerned with the production of oestrogens, thus oestriol (one of the oestrogens produced) is sometimes measured in the maternal urine as a guide to fetal well-being. In cases of fetal adrenal atrophy, which occurs in anencephalic babies (see glossary), the oestrogen excretion is low.

(iii) Human placental lactogen (H P L) is another hormone produced by the placenta. It affects carbohydrate metabolism and is also thought to be concerned with fetal growth. The level of human placental lactogen in maternal blood is one method of assessing placental function, as it normally rises as pregnancy advances.

(*f*) **Barrier.** The placenta acts as a barrier and prevents certain harmful substances passing from the mother to the fetus. It is not a complete barrier, however, since viruses, such as rubella and some other micro-organisms, e g the spirochaete of syphilis, if present in the mother's blood, may cross the placenta and damage the developing fetus. Drugs which cross the placenta may also be harmful to the fetus, though some, such as penicillin, may be beneficial.

Abnormalities of the placenta

Succenturiate lobe. This lobe of placental tissue which is separated from the main placenta, is connected to the placenta by blood vessels which cross the membranes. If these vessels lie in front of the presenting part over the cervical os (a condition known as vasa praevia), they could rupture and the fetus may then be exsanguinated. When examining the placenta and membranes after delivery, the midwife always looks for blood vessels and a small hole in the membranes which could indicate the presence of a succenturiate lobe. If retained in the uterus it might lead to a post-partum haemorrhage.

Bi-partite placenta. A placenta divided into two main lobes.

Circumvallate placenta. A double layer of membrane forming an opaque ring on the fetal surface of the placenta. This seems to be of no harmful significance.

Placental infarcts. These are areas of necrosed (dead) placental tissue which are initially red but later become white, and are caused by interference with the blood supply to the placenta, as occurs, for instance, in the hypertensive conditions. An infarcted placenta may lead to fetal hypoxia because of the reduced amount of functioning placental tissue.

The fetal membranes

The fetus and liquor amnii are enclosed in a double layer of membranes, the amnion and chorion.

The **amnion** is the inner membrane lining the cavity of the uterus and is adherent to the chorion. It can be peeled off the chorion, however, and over the placenta to the umbilical cord. It is a smooth, transparent membrane and is somewhat tougher than the chorion. The amnion secretes the liquor amnii which fills the amniotic cavity.

The **chorion** is the outer membrane attached to the decidua and is continuous with the edge of the placenta. It is a thicker, more opaque membrane and, being more friable than the amnion, is more likely to be retained in the uterus at delivery.

The **liquor amnii** (or amniotic fluid) is the fluid which surrounds the fetus in the uterus. It is a clear, straw-coloured fluid with an alkaline reaction and is composed of nearly 99 per cent. water, the remainder being protein, glucose and various mineral salts, also urea, as the fetus passes urine into the liquor. In addition it contains lanugo (fetal hair), vernix caseosa (see p. 102), and desquamated cells from the fetus and amnion. At term there is about one litre of liquor amnii, but it is being produced continually by the amnion and removed by the fetus because it is swallowed, absorbed into the fetal circulation and carried to the placenta for excretion. The total volume of liquor, therefore, is changed about every three hours, apart from larger particles which remain in the amniotic sac for a longer time.

Functions of the liquor amnii. (1) It allows for the growth and free movement of the fetus in the uterus; (2) it acts as a shock absorber, thereby protecting the fetus from trauma and jarring; (3) it helps to maintain the constant temperature of the fetal environment, and (4) during labour it equalises the pressure on the fetus during uterine contractions and prevents marked interference with the placental circulation.

The umbilical cord

The umbilical cord extends from the fetal surface of the placenta to the fetal umbilicus. At term it is about 50 cm long and 2 cm in diameter; it is composed of connective tissue called Wharton's jelly and is covered with amnion. It contains three fetal blood vessels; the large umbilical vein which carries *oxygenated* blood from the placenta to the fetus, and two umbilical arteries, which twist around the vein in a spiral fashion, and convey *deoxygenated* blood from the fetus to the placenta. These vessels can clearly be seen when the cord is examined after delivery.

Abnormalities of the umbilical cord

If only one umbilical artery is present, this could be associated with a congenital malformation such as renal agenesis (absence of kidneys), and the paediatrician should always be informed.

When the cord is too long it is more likely to prolapse (see p. 156) or become entangled around the fetus; only rarely is it short enough to cause problems, such as delay in descent of the fetus in labour. Occasionally there is a true knot in the cord which, if pulled tight, will cut off the oxygen supply to the fetus. More commonly a false knot is present which is simply extra Wharton's jelly and has no significance. Occasionally the cord is found to be inserted into the edge of the placenta (battledore insertion), or it may even be inserted into the membranes (velamentous insertion). The former is of no consequence, but in the latter case blood vessels from the cord cross the membranes to the placenta and vasa praevia could occur (see p. 39).

The fetal circulation

During intra-uterine life the fetal blood has to circulate through the vessels in the placenta in order to obtain oxygen and food. The circulation consequently follows a different route from that followed in extra-uterine life to ensure that oxygenated blood from the placenta reaches the vital centres with a high oxygen content.

Temporary structures. During fetal life there are five temporary structures in the fetal circulation (see Fig. 13).

(1) The *umbilical vein* which carries oxygenated blood from the placenta to the fetus; it terminates in the fetal liver.

(2) The *ductus venosus*, a branch of the umbilical vein which takes most of the oxygenated blood straight to the inferior vena cava.

(3) The *foramen ovale* between the right and left atria of the heart which allows most of the oxygenated blood in the inferior vena cava to pass from the right to the left atrium into the left ventricle and so to the aorta. Branches from

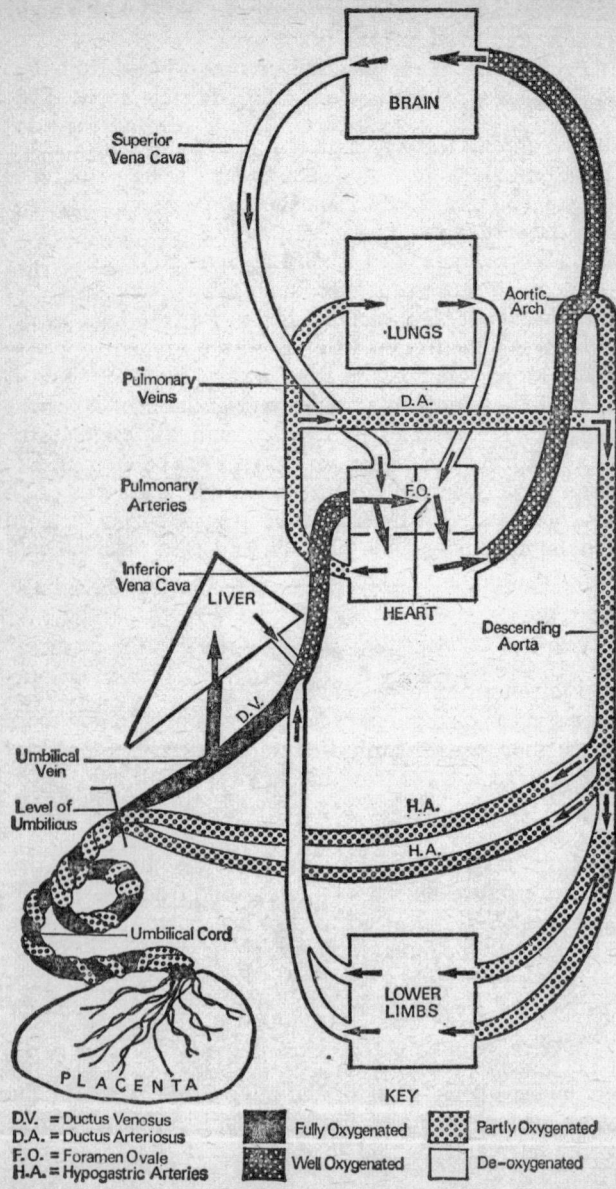

Fig. 13. The fetal circulation.

the arch of the aorta subsequently convey blood with a high oxygen content to supply the brain.

(4) The *ductus arteriosus* which diverts most blood from the pulmonary arteries to the descending thoracic aorta. The lungs require only a small blood supply because they do not function, except to make some rudimentary movements, before birth.

(5) The *hypogastric arteries* which branch from the internal iliac arteries and pass through the umbilicus to become the umbilical arteries in the cord. They convey most of the deoxygenated blood from the upper part of the body back to the placenta for re-oxygenation, as the lower limbs require only a small blood supply.

Changes in the circulation after birth

Several changes occur simultaneously in the minutes following birth, as the baby begins to breathe and the flow of blood from the placenta ceases.

(1) When the cord is ligated, or pulsation ceases, the umbilical vein collapses.

(2) With falling pressure in the umbilical vein, the ductus venosus also collapses.

(3) Because of the decrease in blood flow from the placenta to the inferior vena cava, the pressure in the right atrium of the heart will be reduced, and the foramen ovale will become closed.

(4) As the baby takes its first breath, the lungs expand, the pulmonary vessels dilate, the ductus arteriosus contracts, and blood is diverted into the pulmonary arteries. Blood from the lungs returns to the heart via the pulmonary veins, so increasing the pressure in the left atrium, which assists in the closure of the foramen ovale.

(5) With lack of blood flow through the umbilical cord, the hypogastric arteries thrombose, and become obliterated.

Although these happenings commence very shortly after birth, and the extra-uterine circulation becomes established quickly, the temporary structures remain patent for some time after birth and then most of them eventually become ligaments.

The fetal skull

The fetal skull is the largest and hardest part of the fetus and undergoes considerable pressure during its passage through the birth canal. The vault of the skull is compressible and, when subjected to pressure, changes shape, whereas the bones of the face and the base do not alter.

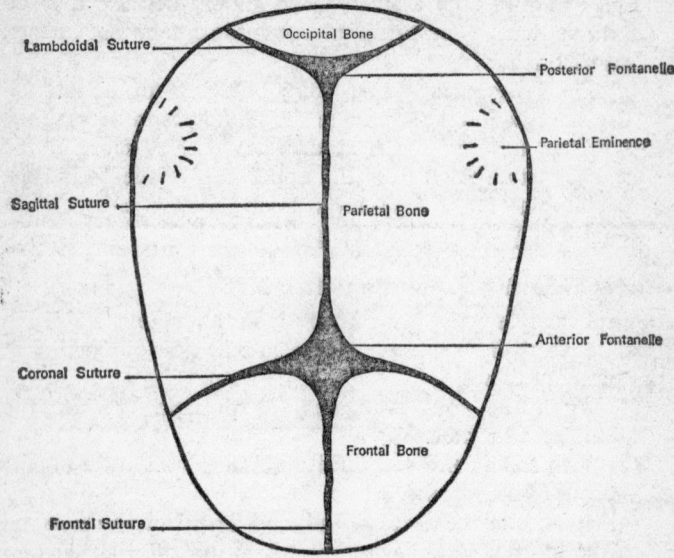

Fig. 14. Bones, sutures and fontanelles of the fetal skull.

The large, compressible vault is composed of the following bones: two frontal, two parietal, and one occipital. The upper part of the two temporal bones also forms part of the vault of the fetal skull. These flat bones are formed from membrane and, because ossification is incomplete at birth, there are membranous spaces called sutures between the bones. There are four sutures:

(1) the *frontal suture* which lies between the two frontal bones and extends from the root of the nose to the anterior fontanelle;

(2) the *sagittal suture* which lies between the parietal bones and extends from the anterior to the posterior fontanelle (sagitta means 'arrow', and the sagittal suture with the anterior and posterior fontanelles forms an arrowlike shape);

(3) the *coronal suture* which lies between the frontal and the parietal bones radiating from either side of the anterior fontanelle (corona means 'crown'); and

(4) the *lambdoidal suture* which lies between the parietal bones and the occipital bone radiating from either side of the posterior fontanelle.

The **fontanelles** are larger membranous spaces where two or more sutures meet. There are six in the fetal skull, but only two are of obstetric significance.

(1) The *anterior fontanelle*, or bregma, is a diamond-shaped area at the junction of the frontal, sagittal and coronal sutures, measuring approximately 4 cm long by 2·5 cm wide. It takes 18 months to close. (Bregma means 'soft', and mothers often refer to the anterior fontanelle as the 'soft spot'.)

(2) The *posterior fontanelle*, or lambda, is a triangular-shaped area, much smaller than the anterior fontanelle, at the junction of the sagittal and lambdoidal sutures. Named after the Greek letter 'lambda' which its shape resembles, it is closed by the 6th to 8th week after birth (see Fig. 14).

Regions of the fetal skull

For descriptive purposes the skull is divided into regions:

the *face* extends from the bridge of the nose to where the chin joins the neck;

the *brow* (or sinciput) is the area from the root of the nose to the anterior fontanelle;

the *vertex* is the area between the anterior and posterior fontanelles and the two parietal eminences: this part of the head is usually delivered first;

the *occiput* extends from the posterior fontanelle to the junction of the head and neck behind.

The measurements of the fetal skull (see Fig. 15)

The diameters of the fetal skull depend on the degree of flexion or extension of the fetal head.

Sub-occipito bregmatic, 9·5 cm. Measured from the junction of the head and neck behind to the middle of the anterior fontanelle, this is the most favourable diameter and presents (together with the bi-parietal, also 9·5 cm) when the head is fully flexed.

Sub-occipito frontal, 10 cm. Measured from the junction of the head and neck to the middle of the frontal suture, this diameter presents when the head is almost fully flexed.

Occipito-frontal, 11·5 cm. Measured from the occipital protuberance to the root of the nose, this is the presenting diameter when the head is deflexed (erect).

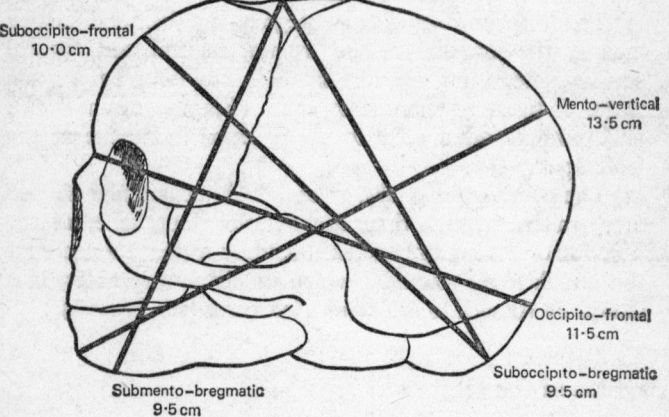

Fig. 15. Diameters of the fetal skull.

Mento-vertical, 13·5 cm. Measured from the tip of the chin to the highest point on the vertex, this diameter presents with the brow presentation when the head is partially extended.

Sub-mento bregmatic, 9·5 cm. Measured from where the chin joins the neck in front to the centre of the anterior fontanelle, this diameter presents in a face presentation when the head is fully extended.

The transverse diameters. There are two transverse diameters: the bi-parietal, 9·5 cm, measured between the parietal eminences, and the bi-temporal, 8·0 cm, measured between the most distant points of the coronal suture.

Circumferences. When the head is fully flexed the sub-occipito bregmatic circumference, measuring 33 cm, enters the pelvic brim. The circumference of a deflexed head is the occipito-frontal and measures 35 cm.

Moulding of the fetal skull

This is the change in shape of the fetal head which occurs during its passage through the birth canal in labour and is due to pressure on the head by the bony pelvis and soft tissues of the birth canal which causes overlapping of the bones of the vault. The frontal and occipital bones slip under the parietal bones and one parietal bone slides under the other. The result of moulding is that the presenting diameter, which is most compressed, is shortened by as much as 1·25 cm, whereas the diameter at right angles is elongated. Normal moulding, such as occurs in a well-flexed head, is not harmful, but moulding which is too rapid, excessive or occurs when the head is not well-flexed may cause cerebral injury.

4. The Physiology and Diagnosis of Pregnancy

Maternal changes in pregnancy

Pregnancy lasts approximately 266 days from conception to birth but, as the time of ovulation cannot be known accurately and usually occurs in mid-cycle, the expected date of delivery is calculated as nine calendar months and seven days from the first day of the last normal menstrual period. Using this means, pregnancy is estimated to last 40 weeks, but being a physiological period subject to variation, any duration between 38 and 42 weeks is considered normal. During this time, certain changes take place in a woman's body, many of them occurring long before abdominal enlargement becomes obvious. All systems of the body are affected to some degree.

Changes in the reproductive organs during pregnancy

The uterus

The uterus grows to a much larger organ in pregnancy and then regresses in the puerperium.

Its *size* increases from 7·5 cm long, 5 cm wide and 2·5 cm deep to 30 cm × 23 cm × 20 cm.

Its *weight* increases from 60 g to 1 kg, mainly due to the enormous growth of the myometrium.

Its *shape* changes from pear-shaped to spherical at eight weeks, to globular at 12 weeks, and to ovoid from 16 weeks.

The *structure*. The endometrium thickens, and is called the decidua, which remains throughout pregnancy, with resultant amenorrhoea, and is shed in the puerperium. Considerable activity occurs in the myometrium. New muscle fibres are laid down, and in addition every existing muscle fibre grows many times in length and thickness. The lower uterine segment forms from the isthmus, enlarging from 7 mm to 7·5 cm. It softens and stretches in the last weeks of pregnancy, helping the presenting part to sink down and engage in the pelvis.

The *cervix* softens and its racemose glands produce a thicker secretion which collects in the cervical canal as a mucoid plug called the operculum. It helps to prevent microorganisms from entering the uterus during pregnancy, and comes away streaked with a little blood when the cervix is taken up at the end of pregnancy or in early labour when it is known as the show.

The *blood supply* to the uterus is considerably increased and the tortuous blood vessels become straighter as the uterus grows and stretches.

Lymph drainage is greater with the increased fluid volume in the uterus.

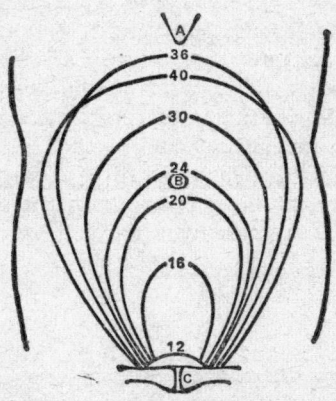

LANDMARKS A — Xiphisternum. B — Umbilicus. C — Symphysis pubis.
Fig. 16. Height of the uterine fundus in pregnancy.

The growth of the uterus. The uterus becomes palpable abdominally after the 12th week of pregnancy. By 16 weeks it is midway between the upper border of the symphysis pubis and the umbilicus, which it reaches at about 20 weeks. At 30 weeks it is midway between the umbilicus and the ensiform cartilage (xiphisternum). At the 36th week of pregnancy, the fundus is usually at the level of the ensiform cartilage, causing a certain amount of dyspnoea. In the last four weeks of pregnancy, as the presenting part enters the pelvis, the fundus becomes lower and at term is about four fingers' breadth below the ensiform cartilage. These levels are a much more useful guide in a primigravida than in a multigravida, but in any patient, her height, general build and muscle tone must also be taken into account. The uterus contracts and relaxes during pregnancy, although the woman may not be aware of the fact. These are called Braxton Hicks contractions and are thought to assist in the circulation of blood to the placental site. They become stronger and more frequent and may cause effacement of the cervix, in the later weeks of pregnancy.

The vagina

The blood supply to the vagina is increased, which has three effects. Firstly, a lilac colouring of the lining, seen on speculum examination; secondly, softening of the tissues to allow easy distension during labour; and thirdly, greater vaginal discharge. In the non-pregnant state the discharge comprises extra-cellular (tissue) fluid from around the muscle walls, desquamated cells containing glycogen from the lining epithelium, and alkaline mucus from the cervix. In pregnancy the fluid and glycogen is increased (an effect of oestrogen), but the operculum remains in the cervix, resulting in a slightly more acid discharge. It is normally white and has an inoffensive odour.

The ovaries

During pregnancy the monthly ripening of a Graafian follicle followed by ovulation ceases, because follicle stimulating hormone is not being produced. The corpus luteum persists and proliferates, producing progesterone and oestrogens until the placenta takes over this function from about the 12th week of pregnancy. The corpus luteum then regresses. The ovaries and Fallopian tubes become abdominal organs as the uterus rises into the abdominal cavity.

The breasts

Breast changes occur in the early weeks of pregnancy due to the influence of the hormones oestrogen and progesterone. The woman may be aware of a tingling prickling sensation in her breasts as early as the third or fourth week of pregnancy. By the sixth week breast enlargement is apparent, due to the growth of the ducts and alveoli, and the breasts are usually firm and tense by this time, with a visible network of surface veins. About the 12th week the nipples and areolae change from pink to a brownish colour, this pigmentation being especially marked in brunettes, but less noticeable in red or fair-haired women. About this time small erections, the openings of sebaceous glands called Montgomery's tubercles, become evident on the primary areola, their function being to secrete sebum to keep the nipple supple. From the 16th week a small amount of fluid, called colostrum, can be expressed from the breasts. At about the 24th week the secondary areola may appear, especially in brunettes, and is recognizable as a mottled zone of pigmentation surrounding the primary areola.

Changes in other parts of the body in pregnancy

The cardio-vascular system

A 30 per cent. increase in blood volume occurs by the 30th week of pregnancy, but there is a greater increase in plasma than in red blood cells, hence the haemoglobin concentration falls. This haemodilution results in physiological anaemia which, unless the woman has an adequate intake of iron, may become worse, because the fetus is withdrawing iron from the mother to supply its daily needs and store in its liver for future use. There is also an increase in the white blood cells and platelets in pregnancy but the hydraemia (relative dilution of the blood) dilutes the plasma proteins, thereby reducing the osmotic pressure and increasing the tendency to oedema.

The veins become relaxed and dilated under the influence of progesterone, thus slowing the return of blood to the heart and increasing the likelihood of varicosities. There is little change in blood pressure, though it tends to become more labile (unstable) and in some women falls slightly in the midtrimester, probably due to the slackened tension in the veins.

The heart is displaced during the later months of pregnancy as the growing uterus pushes the diaphragm upwards. It has to work harder to cope with the increased blood volume and additional weight in pregnancy, but a normal heart easily meets these demands, whereas a diseased heart may fail.

The respiratory system

Oxygen requirements are greater because of increased metabolism, new body tissue and the needs of the fetus. Pregnant women tend to breathe more deeply, therefore increasing their tidal volume (air moved into and out of the lungs with each respiration) and this provides the extra oxygen required. The respiratory rate is little affected until the later part of pregnancy when the uterus pushes the diaphragm upwards, so compressing the bases of the lungs; this results in dyspnoea, which improves as the presenting part becomes engaged in the pelvis causing the fundus to become lower.

The urinary system

The kidneys are required to cope with an increased volume of fluid in pregnancy. The glomerular filtration rate is increased by as much as 60 per cent. and when tubular resorbtion cannot keep pace many substances such as glucose are more readily excreted. Glycosuria therefore occurs fairly commonly in pregnant women due to the lowered renal threshold for sugar.

The renal pelvis and ureters become dilated and tortuous, due to the relaxation of plain muscle and the pressure of the growing uterus on the ureters at the pelvic brim; this results in the slower passage, and often stasis, of urine, and urinary tract infections are more likely. Hormones and the increased vascularity also affect the bladder, and many women have an increased frequency of micturition throughout pregnancy, often with nocturia. This may be particularly troublesome when there is pressure on the bladder as occurs in the first three months when the uterus is enlarging in the pelvis, and in the last month when the presenting part becomes engaged.

The alimentary tract

Smooth muscle throughout the alimentary tract is relaxed due to the action of progesterone, and this causes many of the minor disorders of pregnancy. Heartburn is common because the cardiac sphincter is relaxed, allowing acid stomach contents to regurgitate into the oesophagus. The stomach takes longer to empty and, though the slower passage of food through the alimentary tract encourages more complete absorption of foodstuffs, it also leads to constipation. The cause of nausea and vomiting which often occurs in the early weeks of pregnancy is not fully understood, but it is thought to be at least partially hormonal in origin.

Some pregnant women develop an unexplained craving or distaste for certain foods. This pica, as it is called, may be beneficial if, for instance, an obese woman is unable to take sugar, but it can also be harmful or expensive if it causes compulsive eating of fattening foods, such as potatoes, or a longing for fresh strawberries out of season.

The endocrine system

The thyroid, suprarenal and pituitary glands all enlarge in pregnancy and the secretion of most hormones is increased. There is, however, some doubt about increased thyroid activity, though the metabolic rate is raised. The corpus luteum of the ovary produces oestrogens and progesterone until the placenta takes over this function by the end of the third month of pregnancy. The placenta develops into the largest and most active gland of all during its short life (see p. 38).

The skeletal system

Posture and gait change in pregnancy as the uterus enlarges and, to compensate for the increasing weight in front, the woman tends to lean back, thereby increasing her lumbar curve. Towards the end of pregnancy the pelvic joints relax and this, together with the change in posture, often leads to backache.

The skin

Areas of brown pigmentation develop during pregnancy, especially in brunettes. The aerolae and nipples darken, and the linea alba, the white line between the recti abdominis muscles, becomes the linea nigra. Occasionally blotchy, or freckled, areas appear on the face, and a peculiar marking around the eyes known as the chloasma or mask of pregnancy. The skin of the abdomen, thighs and breasts is very stretched and the deeper layers of the skin may rupture causing striae gravidarum, commonly known as stretch marks. They are red when they first become visible, are pink until the end of pregnancy, then fade to a silvery whiteness, but never completely disappear.

The sweat and sebaceous glands are more active.

The emotions

A woman has more labile emotions in pregnancy and the puerperium than at other times, although she will not change her basic emotional type. Increased hormonal activity makes her more emotional, on top of which are added her thoughts and anxieties about her unborn baby. In early pregnancy, her emotions will tend to be coloured by whether she wanted this pregnancy or not. By mid-pregnancy, her emotions tend to be more stable, and then as labour draws nearer, anticipation mixed with fear often predominates. Emotions must not be confused with thoughts, for a woman often tries to reason herself out of her particular emotional state, but usually with only limited success.

Diagnosis of pregnancy

Many of the changes described cause signs and symptoms which aid the diagnosis of pregnancy.

The **possible signs and symptoms** of pregnancy are usually noted by the patient early in pregnancy:

(1) amenorrhoea
(2) breast changes occur as early as three to four weeks after conception (see pp. 50 & 51 for details)
(3) increased frequency of micturition (see p. 52)
(4) nausea and vomiting (see pp. 53 & 130)
(5) enlargement of the abdomen (see p. 49)
(6) quickening – fetal movement felt by the mother (see pp. 57 & 58)
(7) skin changes (see p. 53).

The **probable signs** of pregnancy are observed by the doctor when he makes an examination per vaginam.

(1) Softening and lilac colouration of the vagina and cervix. The softening may be demonstrated by Hegar's sign in early pregnancy, when on bimanual examination, the

fingers in the vagina and those on the abdomen seem to meet, because the uterine isthmus elongates, is very thin and can hardly be felt in contrast with the relatively bulky cervix and upper uterus.

(2) Enlargement of the uterus.

(3) Internal ballottement elicited after the 16th week of pregnancy when, on giving the uterus a sharp tap with two fingers in the anterior fornix of the vagina, the doctor feels the fetus float away and return with a slight impact on his examining fingers.

(4) Braxton Hicks contractions, the painless, irregular contractions of pregnancy which commence at about the 16th week.

(5) Increased pulsation in the lateral fornices due to the greater blood supply.

The **positive signs** of pregnancy are the fetal heart sounds and the palpation of fetal parts and movements by the examiner. Though the fetal skeleton can be seen on X-ray from the 14th–16th week of pregnancy, X-rays are not taken until after 32 weeks because irradiation may be dangerous to the fetus. Ultrasonography (see p. 183), however, can be used for diagnostic purposes very early in pregnancy.

Pregnancy tests are sometimes carried out to confirm the diagnosis of pregnancy, based on the fact that human chorionic gonadotrophin (H C G) is produced by the placenta and excreted in the maternal urine. In the past, when biological tests were carried out, maternal urine was injected into animals, such as mice, toads or rabbits, and caused changes in their reproductive organs if the urine contained H C G, the test therefore being positive. Nowadays quicker, simpler immunological tests are performed, the results being available within two hours. When urine from a pregnant woman which contains H C G is mixed with serum containing anti-H C G, the H C G in the urine is neutralized. If this urine is then mixed with red blood cells or latex particles coated with H C G, no reaction (haemagglutination) will occur and the pregnancy test is therefore said to be positive. If the woman is not pregnant, agglutination (clumping) of the red blood cells will result, the test therefore being negative. These tests are over 90 per cent. accurate, but when errors do occur, they are mostly false positives.

5. Ante-Natal Care

Ante-natal care started at the beginning of this century. Until then few women received care from a midwife or doctor until the onset of labour. Now all pregnant women are strongly urged to seek early and regular ante-natal supervision, as it has proved to be a vital part of good obstetric care.

Aims

The aims of ante-natal care are to maintain the mother's general health in pregnancy and to detect and treat any complications which might arise. Professional supervision throughout pregnancy, and mental and physical preparation for childbirth, help to achieve a normal labour and delivery of a mature and healthy baby. Subsequently, the mother should make a good recovery, with the successful establishment of breast feeding. Parentcraft classes during the ante-natal period help to prepare the parents for their new role and responsibilities.

Booking

After missing one or two menstrual periods, a woman usually experiences some of the signs and symptoms of pregnancy and should arrange to see her family doctor who will confirm pregnancy and discuss where she is to receive her ante-natal care, have her baby and the probable length of stay in hospital following delivery. He will refer the patient to a hospital ante-natal clinic if she is to have a hospital confinement, but if a general practitioner obstetrician himself, he may wish to share some of her ante-natal care. If the patient is to be booked for home confinement, the community midwife and general practitioner obstetrician will be responsible for her ante-natal supervision.

It is now considered safer for a woman to have her baby in

hospital; thus only a patient in good health, between the ages of eighteen and thirty-five, with no history of medical, obstetric or paediatric complications and having her second or third normal pregnancy, should be considered for home confinement. The home, of course, has to be suitable, and adequate help available for the care of mother and baby.

At the first visit to the ante-natal clinic the patient is welcomed in a friendly way and put at ease. A simple explanation of ante-natal care should be given.

History taking

A detailed history is required and should be taken by the midwife in privacy and in a pleasant, unhurried manner. The information obtained may highlight obstetrical or medical problems which could complicate pregnancy or labour, but it also portrays the woman in the context of her family and her place in society, thus enabling those caring for her to consider her as a whole person.

Social history. Full name, address, telephone number, age, date of birth, religion, occupation, marital status and number of years married are clearly recorded. Marital status is determined because some unsupported mothers may wish to be referred to a social worker. Also, the clinic staff must understand the patient's circumstances if they are to give the help and support which may be needed. The duration of marriage is established, as this occasionally reveals a history of infertility; closer supervision of pregnancy would then be necessary.

History of present pregnancy. The patient is asked how she feels and if she is experiencing any of the symptoms of pregnancy such as nausea and breast discomfort. The date of the first day of the last normal menstrual period is noted, to which seven days and nine calendar months are added to calculate the estimated date of delivery (E D D). It is important to ask if the woman has a regular, twenty-eight-day menstrual cycle, because an irregular cycle will alter the estimated date of delivery. If the patient has been taking oral contraceptives, the E D D may be difficult to forecast, as the time of ovulation is so uncertain. All patients should be asked to note the date when fetal movements are first felt, and this is especially important if there is doubt about the date of the last menstrual period. Primigravidae usually feel movements between 18–20 weeks, whereas multigravidae often recognize the sensation a little earlier, between 16–18 weeks. Any history of bleeding since the last normal menstrual period is noted and the patient asked to seek medical advice immediately should further bleeding occur.

Obstetric history. This is essential, because it may reveal complications which could recur. Information is recorded about all previous pregnancies, including miscarriages, in chronological order. The facts required about each pregnancy include date and place of confinement, duration of pregnancy and labour, method of delivery and any complications which arose in pregnancy, labour or the puerperium. The sex and birthweight of each baby is recorded and the mother asked if the children are well. Any history of obstetric or paediatric complications may prompt the doctor to write to the appropriate hospital for further details. The mother is then asked if she breast fed her babies and a note made of any feeding difficulties. The length of time breast feeding continued and the method of suppression is discussed. The mother who did not breast feed is asked how lactation was suppressed.

Medical history. A detailed medical history is obtained to disclose any conditions which may complicate pregnancy. Patients with medical conditions such as diabetes mellitus, essential hypertension and renal, cardiac or respiratory diseases should have close supervision during pregnancy by an obstetrician and the appropriate physician. The patient is asked if she has had rubella or rubella vaccination and warned to avoid contact with the disease, especially if she has not had the infection, because the virus can damage the developing fetus. Events such as blood transfusions, operations and accidents should be recorded and a special note made if they involve the pelvis or organs of the birth canal. For instance, if a patient has had uterine surgery, there is a slight risk that the scar may rupture as the uterus stretches. Diseases or accidents involving the pelvis may result in a contracted pelvis, which could make vaginal delivery impossible. It is also important to enquire about nervous disorders and depression, because psychiatric conditions may recur in pregnancy or the puerperium. Enquiries about treatment by her doctor or in hospital may help the patient recall some of these facts. The woman is then asked if she smokes. Smoking causes vasoconstriction of the arterioles which results in a diminished supply of food and oxygen to the fetus, and therefore fetal development may be retarded. Hence, smoking is discouraged in pregnancy.

Family history. Finally, the woman is asked about the health of her family, because some diseases, such as hypertension and diabetes, are hereditary. Any history of tuberculosis in the family is relevant because of the infectious nature of the disease; thus it may be necessary to ensure that the patient has a chest X-ray in pregnancy and for the baby to be given a Bacille Calmette Guérin (B C G) vaccination within a few days of birth. It is also of interest to find out if there are twins in the family, as there is a hereditary factor in multiple pregnancies.

Examination

During the history-taking, the midwife observes the patient's general condition, whether she appears well and happy or perhaps pale and worried. As she walks her gait is observed for a limp which could denote a pelvic abnormality. The patient is then weighed and her height is measured; stature (and size of feet) gives some indication of pelvic size.

Weight. Total weight gain in pregnancy should not exceed 12 kg. Only 2–3 kg should be gained in the first 20 weeks and no more than 0·5 kg per week in the latter half of pregnancy. Excessive weight gain may be due to dietary causes or marked fluid retention, which may be a sign of pre-eclampsia (see p. 132); thus it always needs investigation.

Insufficient weight gain may also occur in the later weeks of pregnancy, and usually indicates poor fetal growth due to placental insufficiency. Investigations of placental function and perhaps hospital admission and early induction of labour would then be necessary.

Blood pressure is taken and recorded. The booking blood pressure, if taken in early pregnancy, is important, as it is considered to be the patient's normal blood pressure, and any rise which might occur in later pregnancy could be one of the signs of pre-eclampsia (see p. 132).

Urine. To exclude contamination, the patient is asked to produce a midstream specimen of urine. The colour, odour, reaction and specific gravity of the urine are noted and the specimen is then tested for protein, sugar and ketone bodies in the ante-natal clinic. Proteinuria may be caused by a urinary tract infection or renal disease; later in pregnancy it may be the most serious sign of pre-eclampsia, necessitating immediate admission to hospital. Glycosuria is most likely to be caused by the lowered renal threshold to sugar which occurs in pregnancy, but it could also be a sign of diabetes mellitus. Thus, if glycosuria occurs on two or more occasions during pregnancy, the doctor will usually request a glucose tolerance test. Ketone bodies may be present if the patient is vomiting, and indicate that the vomiting is adversely affecting the patient's general condition and that treatment is necessary. The midstream specimen of urine is then sent to the laboratory for bacteriological examination (over 100 000 bacteria per ml signifies infection). If asymptomatic bacteriuria is diagnosed, the patient must be treated with the appropriate antibiotic, to reduce the risk of pyelonephritis developing later in her pregnancy.

A full medical examination is then carried out by the doctor which includes, particularly, examination of the teeth, breasts, heart, lungs, abdomen and legs. On abdominal examination, the size of the uterus is noted and compared with the period of gestation. An examination per vaginam may then be made to confirm the diagnosis of pregnancy and to note whether the size of the enlarging uterus is compatible with the period of amenorrhoea. During this examination any pelvic tumour (uterine fibroids or ovarian cyst) would be noted, also a smear from the cervix may be taken for cytology to detect pre-cancerous cells. This examination per vaginam may be omitted in early pregnancy if there is a history of recurrent abortions, because the patient could associate the examination with abortion. The patient appreciates being told the doctor's findings following this examination, and especially the fact that pregnancy is confirmed.

After this medical examination, or sometimes later in pregnancy, the doctor will sign a certificate indicating that the patient is fit for inhalational analgesia in labour, provided there are no contra-indications.

Blood investigations

A blood specimen is taken at this first visit to the ante-natal clinic for the following investigations: **A, B, O** and **Rhesus grouping,** because a blood transfusion may be necessary in cases of haemorrhage or very severe anaemia. The blood is examined for the presence of **antibodies, Rhesus antibodies** being particularly noted if the mother is Rhesus negative. In Rhesus negative patients repeat tests for the presence of antibodies are carried out monthly from the 26th week because the placenta becomes a less effective barrier as pregnancy advances and fetal cells are therefore more likely to enter the maternal circulation and stimulate the production of antibodies. **Rubella antibodies** are also noted because, if present, the patient is unlikely to have a recurrence of the disease, whereas the non-immune patient could develop rubella if in contact with the condition. The patient's **haemoglobin** is checked at the first visit and then at monthly intervals from the 26th week until delivery. It is usual for all patients to be given iron and folic acid therapy throughout pregnancy to prevent anaemia. If anaemia develops, further investigations and treatment will be necessary. All patients of African, Asian or Mediterranean origin should have their blood examined for **abnormal haemoglobins** to diagnose sickle-cell disease and thalassaemia (see glossary).

Advice to the pregnant woman

Most women are eager to do what is best for their baby and are given the following advice by the midwife early in pregnancy.

Diet. A good diet is essential for fetal nutrition, to maintain the mother's health and prepare her for breast feeding. An adequate intake of protein is necessary and should be included in the three main meals each day. Foods of high biological value (first-class proteins) are meat, fish, eggs, cheese and milk. At least one pint of milk should be taken daily, as it also provides the best source of calcium required for the formation of strong bones and teeth. Plenty of fresh fruit and vegetables should be included in the diet to ensure sufficient vitamins and minerals and to prevent constipation. Carbohydrates such as bread, cake and potatoes must be restricted because they are fattening, and obesity predisposes to pre-eclampsia. Occasional alcoholic drinks are probably harmless.

Rest. Eight to nine hours in bed at night is recommended and, later in pregnancy, an afternoon rest is advisable.

Exercise. Healthy women can continue with moderate exercise such as walking, swimming and gardening, but strenuous exercise and heavy lifting should be avoided.

Clothes. A well-fitting brassiere should be worn with wide straps which do not cut into the shoulders and deep cups which prevent flattening of the nipples. A front opening is also advisable as it may then be suitable for breast feeding. Occasionally, multiparous women with lax abdominal muscles may need a maternity belt. Otherwise, loose clothes which hang from the shoulders are the most comfortable. High-heeled shoes should be avoided as they pre-dispose to backache.

Hygiene. Personal hygiene is most important in pregnancy because the sweat and sebaceous glands are more active and there is an increased leucorrhoea.

Coitus. If a patient has a history of abortions, she is usually advised to avoid sexual intercourse in the early months of pregnancy, particularly at the time when menstruation would normally occur. It is generally considered that care should be taken in the last month of pregnancy.

Drugs. No drugs should be taken in pregnancy unless prescribed by a doctor because many drugs which are normally considered safe could have a harmful effect on the developing fetus.

Smoking should be discouraged in pregnancy (see p. 59).

Travel. Long distance travel should be avoided in the last six weeks or so of pregnancy because of the risk of premature labour. Most airlines will not carry women after about the 32nd week of pregnancy, and may require a doctor's certificate, stating fitness to travel, for those in the earlier stages. Frequent breaks in long, unavoidable car journeys are advisable to alleviate the discomfort of a sitting position.

Maternity benefits. The Maternity Grant is a lump sum available to all pregnant women on their own or their husband's insurance contributions. It can be paid from nine weeks before the E D D and up to three months afterwards. The

Maternity Allowance is paid only on the woman's insurance contributions, providing certain conditions are fulfilled (see current D H S S pamphlet NI 17A). It is a weekly sum, paid for eighteen weeks, eleven weeks before and seven weeks after the confinement. All pregnant women receive free prescriptions and dental treatment and should be encouraged to attend the dentist in pregnancy; dental treatment is also free for one year after delivery. Free milk and vitamins are available for women in pregnancy if they have two children under five years of age, or are receiving supplementary benefits.

Invitation to classes in preparation for childbirth.
Finally, the woman is invited to attend parentcraft classes with her husband, and asked if she would like to attend relaxation or psycho-physical classes in preparation for childbirth (see pp. 69 & 76).

Frequency of subsequent visits

If all is well, the patient is usually asked to attend the ante-natal clinic every four weeks until the 28th week, then every two weeks until the 36th week and weekly thereafter until the onset of labour.

After the doctor's initial examination, ante-natal care may be supervised by a midwife if all is normal, although the patient should be examined again by a doctor at about the 36th week of pregnancy. The midwife would, of course, refer the patient to the doctor should any deviation from the normal occur when more frequent ante-natal visits or perhaps admission to hospital may be necessary.

Subsequent care

A good relationship should be established between the patient and clinic staff during the ante-natal period. The patient's general condition is assessed at each visit by noting her appearance and asking how she feels, and she should always be given the opportunity to ask questions and discuss her problems.

Routine procedures at each attendance include testing the urine for the presence of protein, glucose and ketone bodies, taking the blood pressure, weighing the patient and examining

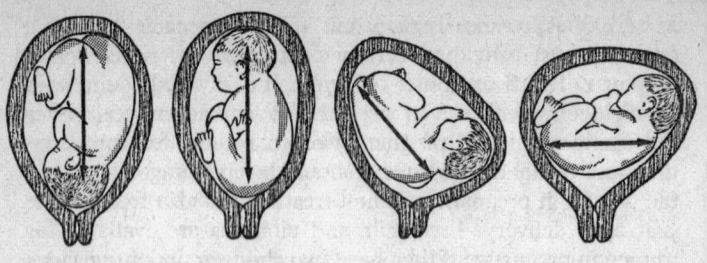

Fig. 17. Lie and presentation of the fetus.

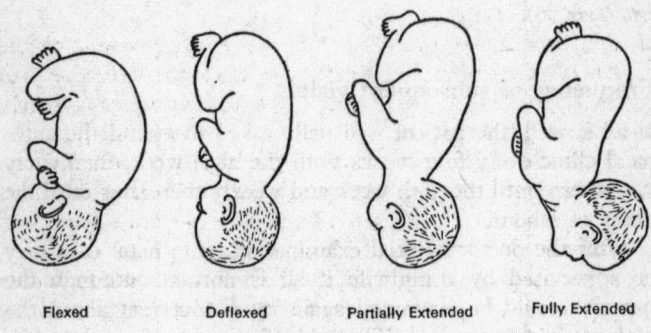

Fig. 18. Attitude of the fetus.

Fig. 19. Positions of the fetus.

her for the presence of oedema. If oedema occurs together with a raised blood pressure and, sometimes, proteinuria, a diagnosis of pre-eclampsia will be made (p. 132). Oedema is most commonly found in the feet, ankles and fingers, but in severe cases facial followed by generalized oedema may occur.

Examination per abdomen

An examination per abdomen is carried out at every clinic visit. Before learning to palpate, however, it is essential to understand the following terms used in relation to the fetus in utero.

1. **Lie** of the fetus is the relationship of the fetal spine to the maternal spine. The normal lie is longitudinal; transverse or oblique lie is abnormal (Fig. 17).
2. **Presentation** is the part of the fetus lying lowest in the uterus. Cephalic (head) presentation is normal after the 34th week of pregnancy; other possible presentations are breech, face, brow and shoulder.
3. **Attitude** is the relationship of the fetal head and limbs to its body. Normally the fetus should be well flexed with its chin on its chest, but the head may be deflexed (erect) or partially or fully extended (Fig. 18).
4. **Denominator** is a part of the presentation used to denote position. The denominator in a cephalic presentation is the occiput, in a breech presentation the sacrum, and in a face presentation the mentum (chin).
5. **Position** is the relationship between the denominator and the mother's pelvis which, for this purpose, is divided into six parts; anterior, lateral and posterior on either side (Fig. 19). Six positions are therefore possible:

1 & 2. Left or right occipito-anterior (L O A or R O A), when the occiput lies in either the left or right anterior section of the mother's pelvis.

3 & 4. Left or right occipito-lateral (L O L or R O L), when the occiput lies in either the left or right lateral section of the mother's pelvis.

5 & 6. Left or right occipito-posterior (L O P or R O P), when the occiput lies in either the left or right posterior section of the mother's pelvis.

6. **Engagement of the head** means that the widest trans-

verse diameter of the fetal head (the bi-parietal diameter, 9·5 cm) has passed through the brim of the pelvis. This usually takes place in a primigravida between the 36th and 38th weeks of pregnancy, but may not occur in a multigravida until labour is established, because of reduced muscle tone in the uterus and abdominal wall.

Method of examination per abdomen

The examination is carried out in privacy with the patient relaxed and comfortable, lying on the couch with one or two pillows under her head and only her abdomen exposed. Her bladder must be empty. The nurse should have clean, warm hands with short nails and stand to the right side of the patient; she should have read the patient's notes. The examination is divided into three parts.

1. **Inspection** to note the size and shape of the abdomen, which should correspond with the period of gestation. Its shape is usually ovoid in a primigravida, whereas it is often round in a multigravida due to lax abdominal muscles. The presence of striae gravidarum (see p. 53), scars, fetal movements and the linea nigra is also noted.

2. **Palpation** may be sub-divided into four parts. Firm but gentle pressure should be exerted, watching the patient's face for any signs of discomfort.

(a) *The height of the uterine fundus* is palpated using the ulnar border of the left hand, and is compared with the size expected for the period of gestation (see Fig. 16). In some centres the distance between the upper border of the symphysis pubis and the uterine fundus is measured at each ante-natal examination to assess fetal growth.

(b) *Pelvic palpation.* The nurse faces the patient's feet and places her hands on each side of the lower abdomen with fingers directed inwards, just above the pelvic brim. Gentle pressure is exerted inwards and downwards, using the pads of the fingers, to feel the presentation. The fetal head feels hard with smooth, rounded contours, and may be ballottable if it is not engaged. Ballottement occurs when the head can be displaced with a sharp tap and is then felt to return against the examining fingers. After 36 weeks engagement of the head should be determined.

(c) *Fundal palpation.* Now the nurse turns to face the patient's head and places both hands on her abdomen, with fingers directed upwards, to palpate the uterine fundus. Usually the softer, irregular outline of the fetal buttocks will be felt, but occasionally the head is located.

(d) *Lateral palpation.* Still facing the patient's head, the right hand is placed flat in order to steady the right side of the abdomen, whilst the fingers of the other hand palpate the left side to try and locate the firm, rounded outline of the fetal back. The process is then reversed and the other side of the abdomen palpated.

3. Auscultation. A Pinard's fetal stethoscope is usually used to listen to the fetal heart which can be heard from about the 24th week of pregnancy. It is most clearly heard if the stethoscope is placed over the back of the fetus. It gives the patient a great thrill to hear her baby's heart beat, using a binaural stethoscope or ultrasonic fetal heart detector.

Until the 32nd week of pregnancy only fetal growth, the presence of fetal movements and fetal heart sounds are important on examination per abdomen. However, from the 32nd week, the lie and presentation should also be determined, as the doctor may wish to correct the presentation, if it is not cephalic. From the 36th week of pregnancy onwards, engagement of the head is particularly noted. If the head is not engaged in a primigravida or cannot be made to engage in a multigravida at 36 weeks, the midwife would refer the patient to the doctor. The doctor usually makes an examination per vaginam to assess the size and shape of the pelvis at about the 36th week, the examination being particularly important with a non-engaged head. If there is any suspicion of cephalopelvic disproportion, the doctor will request a lateral X-ray pelvimetry which shows the antero-posterior diameters and shape of the pelvis and the size of the fetal head. He will then decide if the fetal head is likely to pass through the pelvis and the patient to have a vaginal delivery, or whether a Caesarean section will be necessary.

Breast care

At the patient's first or second clinic attendance the midwife will ask if she has considered how she is going to feed her baby, and will then discuss the advantages and disadvantages of breast and artificial feeding (see Chapter 8).

Examination. The breasts are examined, noting especially their size, shape and enlargement in the early weeks of pregnancy. Normal enlargement is a two-inch increase in total bust measurement; less than this suggests the possibility of poor milk production and three inches or more excessive milk production. Skin texture is next observed: thin, elastic skin stretches easily to accommodate the milk, whereas thick, inelastic skin may lead to discomfort when the breasts fill. Pigmentation of the skin is noted, because fair skinned women with poor pigmentation of the areolae have a tendency to develop sore nipples when breast feeding. Finally, the protraction of the nipples is observed. If protraction is poor or the nipples are fibrous, the baby will have difficulty in grasping the nipple to suck. To improve protraction, glass shells are fitted over the nipples before the 20th week and worn for gradually increasing periods daily, until they are worn all day from the 28th week until term. If overfilling, sore nipples or difficulty in fixing the baby at the breast are likely to mar the early days of breast feeding, there should be a clear indication in the patient's notes that problems may arise. Special steps can then be taken after delivery to minimize these difficulties.

Advice. The patient is advised to wash her breasts daily, taking particular care to remove any dried colostrum from the nipples. Colostrum is secreted by the breasts during pregnancy, and there is often some leakage. If the nipples become dry, a lanolin-based cream can be applied. A well-fitting brassiere should be worn to provide good support. At the 34th week of pregnancy, the breasts are reassessed and the patient may be taught how to massage them gently and express colostrum. Breast massage helps to clear the lactiferous ducts and ensure a good flow of milk after delivery; it should be carried out daily, preferably in the bath, using soap to lubricate the hands. Some people hold that breast massage may damage the tissues, which could then become infected, but if it is done gently this should not occur. If the patient has a history of breast infection, specimens of colostrum are obtained for culture and sensitivity testing. The appropriate antibiotics will be prescribed if pathogenic micro-organisms are shown to be present, and repeat specimens of colostrum are tested on completion of the antibiotic course. Thus, with good ante-natal preparation, the woman may look forward, with confidence, to successful breast feeding.

Preparation for childbirth

Attendance at classes of preparation for childbirth will help both the woman and her husband to understand and cope with the physical and emotional changes of pregnancy, labour and the puerperium. Here the patient will be taught the process of labour, relaxation and the control of breathing so that she can approach her labour with increased confidence. A film showing the birth of a baby may be included in the programme, and the parents will usually be taken to see the labour and post-natal wards, so that the surroundings will be familiar when the woman is eventually admitted. The equipment for inhalational analgesia will be demonstrated and the patient encouraged to practise its use.

Teaching on the development of the baby, preparation for his arrival, infant feeding and general care is given and, in many classes, wider topics such as relationships within the family, and family planning, may also be discussed.

Some patients may not attend the classes of preparation for childbirth; it is therefore essential in such cases to ensure that they will receive adequate information and instruction during their routine ante-natal care.

6. Normal Labour: Physiology and Management

Labour is the process by which the fetus, placenta and membranes are expelled through the birth canal. This normally takes place at term, that is between the 38th and 42nd weeks of pregnancy, but the process is called labour if it occurs at any time after the 28th week.

Labour is divided into 3 stages.

The first stage begins with regular, uncomfortable contractions and the onset of cervical dilatation and is completed with full dilatation of the cervix.

The second stage is the period from full dilatation of the cervix until the birth of the baby.

The third stage begins immediately after the birth of the baby and is completed with the delivery of the placenta and membranes.

The first stage of labour

This is the longest stage of labour and is normally completed in 12–18 hours in primigravidae and 6–12 hours in mu'tigravid patients, although nowadays with the active management of labour (see p. 155) few patients, including primigravidae, are in labour for more than 12 hours.

The signs of labour

1. **Contractions.** Labour begins with uncomfortable, rhythmic uterine contractions which are infrequent at first and may be felt by the woman as tightenings or backache. They become progressively longer, stronger and more frequent as labour progresses.
2. **The show.** For many women the show is the first sign of labour and is recognised as a mucoid, slightly blood-stained vaginal loss.
3. **Rupture of the membranes.** When the membranes rupture there may be an unmistakable gush or just a slight trickle of liquor. It is not a true sign of labour unless it is accompanied by uterine contractions and cervical dilatation.

4. **Dilatation of the cervix** occurs in true labour.

Physiology of the first stage of labour

Two main processes take place during the first stage of labour, (a) effacement of the cervix, and (b) dilatation of the cervical os.
Effacement, or taking up, of the cervix may start at the end of pregnancy but the process is completed in labour. The cervix first becomes shorter and then the internal os opens and merges into the lower segment of the uterus (see Fig. 20).

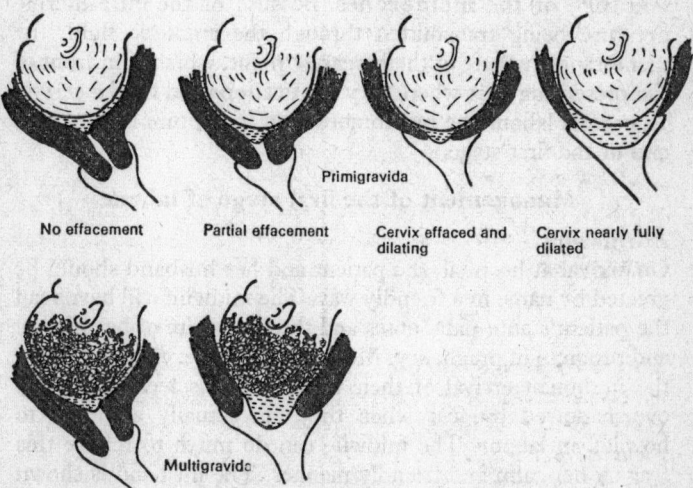

Fig. 20. Effacement and dilatation of the cervix.

Dilatation of the external os then occurs; it is fully dilated when it is approximately 10 cm across, but this depends on the size of the presenting part.

In multigravidae these two processes, effacement and dilatation, may occur simultaneously.

Uterine contractions are responsible for achieving effacement and dilatation of the cervix. The upper segment of the uterus contracts powerfully and retracts, whereas the lower segment is passive and simply distends and dilates. Retraction is a special property of uterine muscle and means that the fibres become a little shorter with each contraction due to their incomplete relaxation. The cavity of the uterus is therefore continually becoming smaller, hence the fetus is forced down onto the cervix which gives way, i e dilates, under the increasing pressure. The upper and lower segments of the uterus function rhythmically together in normal labour and this is called polarity.

The show. In early labour, when the cervix begins to dilate, the woman will usually notice the show. This is the passage of the plug of mucus, called the operculum, which has filled the cervical canal throughout pregnancy.

Rupture of the membranes. Because of the intra-uterine pressure being transmitted through the amniotic fluid, the membranes rupture at their weakest point, which is in front of the presenting part where they are unsupported by the cervix. In normal labour the membranes tend to rupture towards the end of the first stage.

Management of the first stage of labour

Admission

On arrival at hospital, the patient and her husband should be greeted by name in a friendly way. The midwife will have read the patient's ante-natal notes and thus be aware of her history and progress in pregnancy. Most women feel excitement about the imminent arrival of their baby, but this feeling is often overshadowed by fear when they are actually admitted to hospital in labour. The midwife can do much to relieve this fear by her calm and friendly manner. The husband is shown to a visitors' room where he can wait until his wife has been admitted.

Immediate assessment. The midwife quickly assesses the progress of labour by observing the patient's demeanour and obtaining a history, asking when contractions started and about their strength and frequency; she carefully observes the contractions and also the patient's reaction, whether she is relaxed or appears distressed. The patient is asked if she has had a show and whether her membranes have ruptured, and if she is wearing a sanitary pad, this will be inspected for evidence of liquor or possible bleeding.

General examination. The patient then undresses and puts on a clean gown. She is asked for a midstream specimen of urine which is tested for protein and ketone bodies. The patient next lies on the couch, where her temperature, pulse and blood pressure are taken and recorded, and she is examined for the presence of oedema and varicose veins and asked if she has been in contact with or has had any recent infection. It is necessary occasionally to isolate a patient to prevent cross infection in a maternity unit.

An examination per abdomen is next carried out, for it is essential to ensure that the lie is longitudinal and to determine the presentation and position of the fetus. Engagement of the head is also noted and the fetal heart rate is counted.

An examination per vaginam now follows to diagnose the progress of labour. This is an aseptic procedure which is carried out gently by the doctor or the midwife.

Preparation. The vulval and perineal areas may be shaved and, if the patient has not had a good bowel action that day, she is given suppositories, or perhaps an enema, provided delivery is not imminent. A full rectum may delay the descent of the presenting part, and in the second stage of labour faeces will be expelled when the woman is pushing; this is not only a source of embarrassment to her, but increases the risk of infection to both mother and baby. Finally, the woman has a warm bath or shower, which is relaxing and ensures that she is as clean as possible for the delivery of her baby, and she is then transferred to the room which has been prepared for her. In early labour, and if the membranes are intact, the patient may remain up until contractions are stronger, but if the membranes have ruptured, she should stay in bed to reduce the risk of cord prolapse (see p. 156). When the patient is settled in her room, her husband, who will have been kept informed of his wife's progress, may join her.

Nursing care

Emotional care

Emotional support is a vital aspect of care in labour. Most women feel frightened, and the midwife can do much to alleviate this by an understanding and competent manner. Companionship in labour is important, too. More husbands now stay with their wives, but the midwife should be present to reassure them both. Women who have attended preparatory classes are encouraged to carry out their breathing patterns and relaxation; others are taught to breathe correctly as labour progresses. The husband's help is often invaluable here. A simple explanation is given of all procedures carried out during labour and the patient and her husband are kept informed of progress.

Physical care

Posture. Most women find a semi-recumbent position comfortable. They should be well supported with pillows and helped to change their position at intervals. Placental circulation is improved when the patient lies on her side, thus prolonged periods in the dorsal position should be avoided.

Nutrition. Fluids only are given because the stomach empties very slowly in labour and thus, should an anaesthetic become necessary, vomiting may occur which could lead to the acid-aspiration syndrome (Mendelson's syndrome, p. 162). To minimize this risk, patients in labour are given 15 ml of magnesium trisilicate at two hourly intervals to reduce the acidity of the stomach contents. If the woman shows signs of becoming dehydrated or ketotic, an intra-venous infusion of dextrose is given to provide the megajoules (calories) required for the great muscular effort of labour.

Urinary output. The woman should be encouraged to pass urine every two to three hours, as a full bladder not only adds to the discomfort of labour, but may also delay progress. Each specimen of urine is measured and tested for protein and ketone bodies. A trace of protein may be due to contamination by liquor amnii or blood. If the patient is unable to empty her bladder, it will be necessary to pass a catheter.

Hygiene and comfort. Most patients in labour become hot and perspire, and therefore will appreciate a refreshing wash at intervals. Regular vulval washes, given about four- to six-hourly, will keep the patient comfortable and the area clean to help prevent infection. The bed linen should be kept smooth and may need frequent changing if liquor is draining. Mouth care is necessary for the patient is not eating; she will also appreciate having her hair combed occasionally.

Prevention of infection. Preventing infection of the genital tract is an important aspect of care throughout labour. The risk of infection is increased once the membranes have ruptured; attendants should wear masks when the vulva is exposed and wash their hands before caring for the patient. The vulva is covered with sterile pads which are changed frequently, and particular care is taken to prevent the introduction of infection when making examinations per vaginam and at the time of delivery.

Observations

Observations of maternal and fetal conditions are carried out and recorded at regular intervals throughout labour, and any deviation from normal is immediately referred to a doctor. **Pulse** and **blood pressure** are taken at increasingly frequent intervals as labour progresses and the **temperature** is checked four-hourly because of the risk of infection. All **intake and output** is recorded on a fluid-balance chart. The strength, frequency and duration of the uterine **contractions** is carefully observed. To feel contractions, the fingers are placed lightly over the fundus. At the onset of the contraction the fundus becomes hard, a few seconds before the patient is aware of any discomfort; the hardness is accentuated as the intensity of the contraction increases. The duration of contractions is timed by gently feeling the fundus throughout the length of each contraction. Early in labour contractions last about 30 seconds, but as labour advances they become longer, until at the end of the first stage they last for about 60 seconds. The frequency of contractions is assessed by timing the period from the onset of one contraction to the onset of the next. The uterus should relax between each contraction to allow the placental circulation to be resumed, otherwise fetal hypoxia will occur. The nurse should also observe the patient's reaction to contractions, whether she is coping well or showing signs of distress, so that analgesia may be given when required.

Loss per vaginam is observed and the time recorded when the membranes rupture. Clear liquor is normal; meconium-stained liquor is a greenish colour and usually indicates fetal distress. A mucoid, slightly blood-stained show is normal, but any bleeding is abnormal.

The fetal heart must be carefully monitored throughout labour. In many labour wards continuous fetal heart monitoring equipment is now available. Where this is not the case, the fetal heart is checked with a Pinard's fetal stethoscope or an ultrasonic fetal heart detector at increasingly frequent intervals until, at the end of the first stage, recordings are made every 15 minutes. The normal fetal heart rate is between 120 and 160 beats per minute but this is a wide range and a change in rate of about 20 beats per minute or more should lead to closer observation, as it might indicate fetal distress. Any irregularity of the fetal heart beat is also abnormal. Slowing of the fetal heart rate with contractions may be due to compression of the fetal head, but slowing at the end or just after contractions indicates fetal hypoxia. The doctor may then take a blood sample from the fetal scalp for pH estimation (see glossary). The normal pH of fetal blood is 7·35, but if it is below 7·25 immediate delivery will be necessary to prevent damage to the brain cells.

Relief of pain in labour

Early in the first stage the woman is encouraged to read or sew, because activities such as these help to distract her thoughts from the discomfort of labour. Good nursing care does much to relieve the minor discomforts she experiences, and as the first stage progresses, the patient will need the constant support of her midwife as well as her husband to help overcome fear and tension. If she has attended ante-natal classes, she should be encouraged to carry out her breathing patterns and relaxation.

Psychoprophylaxis

This is a method of minimizing pain in labour by ante-natal teaching about (*a*) the process of labour, and (*b*) muscular control. Distractive therapy is used, the patient learning to concentrate on humming or tapping a tune, or lightly massaging the abdomen with her finger tips (effleurage), thereby becoming less aware of her contractions. Breathing patterns vary, but they usually start with deep breathing at the onset of the contraction and gradually change to shallow breathing as the intensity of the contraction increases, then, when the contraction fades, revert to deep breathing again. A modified form of psychoprophylaxis is now being taught in many centres, called *psycho-physical* preparation for childbirth. This involves simpler patterns of breathing, but the mother is still encouraged to concentrate on something other than her contractions. Many women who practise these methods of pain relief require no analgesic drugs and find labour a more pleasurable, fulfilling experience.

Drugs

Many drugs are available nowadays for the relief of pain in labour.

Hypnotics such as dichloralphenazone (Welldorm) 650–1300 mg or nitrazepam (Mogadon) 10 mg may be given very early in labour to induce sleep, as the mother who is well rested usually copes better in advanced labour.

Analgesics. The most widely used drug for the relief of pain in labour is pethidine 50–150 mg, administered intramuscularly. Besides being a powerful analgesic, it also has some antispasmodic action, but does not reduce uterine contractions. However, it does cross the placenta and will depress the fetal respiratory centre and thus is not normally given within about three hours of delivery because it may delay the start of breathing when the baby is born.

Tranquillizers, such as promethazine (Phenergan) 25–50 mg or promazine (Sparine) 25–50 mg are often given together with pethidine because they potentiate (increase) its action. In addition, tranquillizers reduce the incidence of vomiting and relieve anxiety, thus enabling the patient to relax more easily.

Inhalational analgesics. The end of the first stage is usually the most painful part of labour, and it is then that inhalational analgesia is often administered by the midwife to give relief, Entonox, a 50 : 50 mixture of nitrous oxide and oxygen given from an Entonox machine, being widely used for this purpose. Other inhalational analgesics are trichlorethylene (Trilene) 0·35 or 0·5 per cent. mixed with air in a Tecota mark VI or Emotril apparatus, and methoxyflurane (Penthrane) 0·35 per cent. mixed with air in the Cardiff inhaler. Most patients will have seen and practised using the apparatus during the antenatal period and thus it will be familiar when offered in labour. The patient holds the mask over her face and inhales the gas throughout the length of each contraction; between contractions she removes the mask and breathes normally.

Epidural analgesia. An increasing number of women in labour now have epidural analgesia, which blocks the nerves supplying the birth canal and thus relieves the pain of labour and delivery.

Procedure. The patient lies curled up in the position for lumbar puncture and a doctor, usually an experienced anaesthetist, infiltrates the skin and subcutaneous tissues with local anaesthetic and then passes a Tuohy needle into the epidural space under strict aseptic conditions. After aspirating and giving a test dose, the doctor injects 20–30 ml of a local anaesthetic such as bupivacaine (Marcain) 0·25 or 0·5 per cent. (i e 50–75 mg) into the epidural space. If further doses of local anaesthetic are likely to be required, a plastic catheter is threaded through the needle and left in situ so that when the pain returns, top-up doses can be given by the doctor, or a midwife who has been trained in this technique.

Aftercare. After the injection, the patient should lie on her back for about 20 minutes to encourage even distribution of the local anaesthetic, but she should then be turned on her side to avoid the supine hypotensive syndrome. Hypotension is a common complication following epidural analgesia and, therefore, the blood pressure must be recorded at five-minute intervals for twenty minutes after injection, and thereafter, if satisfactory, at fifteen-minute intervals. It is important to realize that patients do not feel their contractions following epidural analgesia and, therefore, contractions must be assessed by careful abdominal palpation. The patient may also be unaware of a full bladder and thus needs to be encouraged at intervals to pass urine; if this is unsuccessful, it will be necessary for her to be catheterized. It should also be realised that because the patient in the second stage of labour is unaware of her contractions, she may not push so effectively and thus could require forceps delivery.

Assessment of progress in labour

Progress in labour is assessed by the following criteria.

(a) Uterine contractions. In normal labour contractions become progressively stronger, longer and more frequent, until at the end of the first stage they are very strong, last about 60 seconds and occur every two or three minutes.

(b) Descent of the presenting part. Descent should occur throughout labour and is assessed by examinations per abdomen and per vaginam. This is a particularly important observation if the head is not engaged at the beginning of labour.

(c) Loss per vaginam. This gives some indication of progress, in that the membranes tend to rupture spontaneously at the end of the first stage, although nowadays they are often ruptured artificially by the doctor or midwife earlier, as this accelerates progress. Towards the end of the first stage, the patient also tends to have a heavier mucoid, slightly blood-stained show.

(d) Dilatation of the cervix. Progress is estimated when making examinations per vaginam every four to six hours, and may be plotted on a partograph chart. Cervical dilatation occurs rather slowly in the early first stage and this is known as the latent phase; when the cervix is effaced (see p. 71) and about 4 cm dilated, progress becomes much quicker and is thus called the accelerated phase. Full dilatation occurs when the cervix is dilated sufficiently to allow the fetal head to pass through, usually to about 10 cm in diameter.

The second stage of labour

This is the period from full dilatation of the cervical os until the fetus has been completely expelled, and lasts for up to one hour in a first labour and up to half an hour in subsequent deliveries.

Physiology of the second stage of labour

At the onset of the second stage of labour the contractions become expulsive in action; they are stronger and longer than in the first stage and last for at least one minute. The diaphragm and abdominal muscles now begin to contract involuntarily and assist the uterus in the expulsion of the fetus, this action being enhanced by the mother actively bearing down in response to a strong desire to push.

As the second stage progresses, the pelvic floor is displaced by the advancing fetus. The vagina is greatly distended as the fetus descends and anteriorly the pelvic floor is pushed up and the bladder rises into the abdomen; posteriorly it is pushed down in front of the presenting part, the rectum being compressed and the perineal body flattened until it is elongated to about 10 cm and is wafer thin.

The fetal head is seen at the vulva with each contraction; between contractions it recedes until the head is crowned, that is when the parietal eminences have been born. The occiput has by then passed under the pubic arch and can no longer slip back, hence the head is born. With the next contraction the remainder of the baby is delivered, thereby completing the second stage of labour.

The mechanism of labour

As the fetus is forced by uterine contractions down the birth canal during the second stage, it undergoes a series of passive movements which are called, collectively, the 'mechanism of labour'; there is a mechanism for every presentation and position which is capable of being delivered vaginally. These movements, being spontaneous, are independent of outside assistance and must not be confused with the method of delivery. The person delivering the baby needs to understand the mechanism in order to anticipate the next movement, and to assist if necessary.

As the commonest position at delivery is the *left occipito-anterior*, its mechanism will now be described in detail:

the *lie* is longitudinal

the *attitude* is one of good flexion

the *presentation* is the vertex

the *presenting part* is the right parietal bone (i e the part of the fetus which is over the internal os)

the *denominator* is the occiput

the *position* is left occipito-anterior

the *engaging diameter* is the sub occipito-bregmatic, 9·5 cm

The movements are as follows:

1. With contractions and retraction of the uterus, increased flexion of the head occurs and descent takes place.
2. The occiput reaches the pelvic floor first and rotates forwards through one eighth of a circle (45°).
3. The occiput is pushed under the pubic arch.
4. The head is crowned (i e the bi-parietal diameter is born).
5. The head extends, the sinciput, face and chin are born.

6. The head restitutes (i e the neck untwists, so that the head is again in the left occipito-anterior position).
7. The anterior shoulder reaches the pelvic floor and rotates forwards through one eighth of a circle.
8. With internal rotation of the shoulders, there is external rotation of the head.
9. The anterior shoulder is pushed under the pubic arch.
10. The posterior shoulder is born.
11. The body is born by lateral flexion (i e a continuation of the curve of the birth canal).

Management of the second stage of labour

Diagnosis

The external signs of full dilatation indicate that the patient is probably in the second stage of labour. One of the earliest of these signs is the patient's desire to push with expulsive contractions. The anus will dilate with contractions and the perineum becomes thin and bulges as it is distended by the presenting part. Finally, the vaginal orifice gapes and the presenting part becomes visible. When the first of these signs appears, the doctor or midwife will usually make an examination per vaginam to confirm full dilatation of the cervix. No cervix will be felt; this is the positive sign of the onset of the second stage.

Nursing care

The patient should be told that she is in the second stage of labour and that this means her baby is ready to be pushed out and will soon be born. The second stage involves hard physical exertion, but it may also be an exciting time, especially when the head becomes visible and the patient can be told such details as the colour of her baby's hair. From now on the midwife will stay with the patient the whole time, and a quiet, calm approach is very reassuring to both the patient and her husband. The patient should be encouraged to pass urine at the onset of the second stage, if she has not recently emptied her bladder, because a full bladder may delay progress, and it may also be damaged by the persistent pressure of the hard fetal head. When the patient has the desire to push, she is encouraged to bear down with each contraction. Instructions are given quietly between contractions. Most patients push more effectively in a semi-recumbent position with head forward and knees well apart, sometimes drawn up towards their chest and supported with hands under the thighs. The patient takes about two deep breaths at the onset of each contraction, using the inhalational analgesia if she wishes, and then holds her breath and pushes down. It is usually possible to achieve two or three long, strong pushes with each contraction. Between contractions she rests and relaxes. This stage of labour is very strenuous for primigravidae and they should be praised for their efforts. Multigravidae may deliver very quickly, sometimes after only two or three expulsive contractions, and, therefore, immediate preparations should be made for delivery.

The patient will appreciate having her face sponged with a cool flannel as she becomes very hot during the exertions of this stage. Sips of iced water are very acceptable. If oral fluids have to be withheld because an anaesthetic may become necessary, mouthwashes can be offered. A vulval wash is given before delivery and the vulva covered with sterile pads between contractions, until delivery is imminent.

Observations

Frequent observations of fetal and maternal condition are made, as in the first stage of labour. Fetal heart recordings are especially important, as fetal distress occurs more commonly in the second stage of labour; thus if continuous fetal heart monitoring is not in use, the fetal heart should be checked towards the end of every contraction. The midwife observes progress by noting the advance of the fetal head. As in the first stage, progress may be rather slow initially, especially in primigravidae, but accelerates towards the end of the second stage.

Preparation for delivery

The room in which the patient is to be delivered should be clean and warm, and it is also important to ensure that the patient has privacy for the birth of her baby. A sterile delivery trolley is prepared, including sterile gown and gloves for the midwife who is to deliver the baby. An oxytocic drug (see glossary) such as Syntometrine 1 ml, is drawn up into a syringe and checked by the midwife. The baby's cot should be warmed, a mucus extractor and oxygen apparatus prepared, and the equipment for intubating the baby also checked in readiness for emergency resuscitative measures.

Delivery

The patient may be delivered in the dorsal or left lateral position. The midwife washes her hands and puts on a sterile gown and gloves. A second nurse supervises the patient taking the inhalational analgesia and quietly relays the midwife's instructions to her. The midwife swabs the vulva with an antiseptic such as chlorhexidine lotion 500 mg in 1 000 ml (1 : 2 000 solution) and then an antiseptic cream. Sterile towels cover the delivery area and a sterile pad is placed over the anus. The midwife maintains her good rapport with the patient and gives instructions in a quiet, unhurried manner. As the head distends the perineum, the midwife may decide that an episiotomy is necessary to prevent a perineal laceration. This is a surgical incision into the perineum to enlarge the vaginal orifice. The doctor or midwife infiltrates the perineum with 10 ml of a local anaesthetic, such as lignocaine 0·5 per cent. (i e 50 mg) and the episiotomy is performed. The midwife then places her hand on the fetal head to maintain flexion and control the delivery, and the patient is asked to breathe steadily in and out as the head crowns. Then the head is extended to allow the face to slip over the perineum. The midwife immediately feels to see if the cord is round the baby's neck; if so, it may be possible to slip it over the baby's head, otherwise it is clamped with two pairs of artery forceps about three to four centimetres apart, cut between them and unwound. Mucus is gently removed from the baby's nose and mouth and the eyes are swabbed. Some mothers like to be propped up to see their baby's head at this stage and perhaps to watch the rest of the delivery.

With the next contraction the baby's body is born, and as the anterior shoulder is delivered the mother is given an intramuscular injection of the oxytocic drug, usually Syntometrine 1 ml, which was prepared earlier. The posterior shoulder is then delivered, followed by the trunk, which is directed towards the mother's abdomen. The midwife notes the time of delivery and tells the parents the sex of their baby. She holds the baby in a head down position to allow drainage of mucus and liquor from the air passages and an assistant clears the pharynx and nostrils with a sterile mucus extractor. The baby is placed on a sterile towel on the bed and the cord is clamped with two pairs of artery forceps about ten centimetres from the umbilicus and cut between the clamps. He is then wrapped in a sterile towel and shown to his parents. If he is pink and crying, the mother may now hold her baby in her arms for a few moments. This is a very joyous occasion and the parents are congratulated on the birth of their child.

The third stage of labour

The third stage covers the period from the birth of the baby until the placenta and membranes are expelled. With the routine administration of an oxytocic drug (see p. 181), usually given as the baby is born, it is normally completed within about five minutes, but if no oxytocic drug has been given the third stage may last for about twenty minutes.

Physiology of the third stage of labour

Two main physiological processes take place during the third stage of labour: (*a*) the separation of the placenta and membranes from the uterine wall, and (*b*) the control of bleeding from the placental site.

Separation of the placenta and membranes takes place because the uterus contracts and retracts powerfully as the baby is delivered and there is a marked reduction in its size and hence in the size of the placental site. This causes the placenta, which does not reduce in size, to peel off the uterine wall, leaving behind many torn maternal blood vessels. With further contractions the placenta descends into the vagina, with the membranes trailing behind.

The control of bleeding is achieved by the powerful contraction and retraction of the uterus following the separation of the placenta, and especially by the action of the interlacing spiral muscles fibres which act as 'living ligatures' by constricting the blood vessels running through the myometrium.

When the uterus is empty and firmly contracted, its walls are pressed together in close apposition, thus exerting pressure on the bleeding points which further aids the control of bleeding. Finally the blood in the torn uterine vessels clots, but this takes some minutes and it is still essential that the uterus remains well contracted to control bleeding.

Management of the third stage of labour

The third stage is the most dangerous time for the woman in labour, for complications such as haemorrhage can occur with alarming rapidity and transform what was a normal labour into a grave emergency. The dangers of shock and haemorrhage can be minimized by good care and management in pregnancy and in labour, so that the patient enters the third stage fit and well prepared, and not anaemic, exhausted or dehydrated, nor with a full bladder.

The patient should be in the dorsal position for the third stage of labour. The midwife rinses her hands in antiseptic lotion and places a receiver between the patient's legs to collect any blood escaping from the vulva. A sterile towel is placed over the mother's abdomen and the midwife then palpates the uterus to ensure that it is well contracted. With active management of the third stage, that is, by giving the mother an oxytocic drug during the delivery of her baby, as already described, the uterus contracts more powerfully, thus speeding up placental separation and reducing blood loss. Having ensured that the uterus is well contracted, active management is continued as controlled cord traction is employed to deliver the placenta. The midwife places her left hand on the lower part of the abdomen, just above the symphysis pubis, to support the uterus, whilst with her right hand she applies steady, sustained traction on the cord in a downward direction. When the placenta becomes visible, the cord is lifted up and the placenta is caught in the cupped hands as it emerges from the vagina. This prevents the membranes from tearing. With this active management of the third stage, the placenta and membranes are usually delivered within about five minutes of the birth of the baby. However, with passive management, which is rarely carried out these days, no oxytocic drug is given during the delivery of the baby and, therefore, placental separation and descent take longer, about 20 minutes. During this time the midwife stands with her left hand resting gently on the fundus to ensure that the uterus remains contracted and does not become soft and enlarged, indicating that it is filling up with blood. When the placenta has separated from the uterine wall and descended into the lower segment, the following signs will be apparent:

the cord lengthens

the fundus rises, but is smaller, very hard and mobile

a small blood loss may accompany the above signs.

The placenta can now be delivered, provided the uterus is well contracted. The mother is encouraged to push, as she did in the second stage, to expel the placenta. If maternal effort fails, the midwife may use her left hand to apply fundal pressure in a downward and backward direction to deliver the placenta.

Care of the mother after delivery

As soon as the placenta is delivered the midwife palpates the uterus to ensure that it is well contracted and observes any blood loss trickling from the vagina. If the uterus is not well contracted, she massages the fundus with her fingers to make it contract and applies fundal pressure to expel any blood clots. It may be necessary to repeat the oxytocic drug if the uterus fails to contract after this treatment.

The vulva and perineum are then gently swabbed with a warm, antiseptic lotion and, together with the lower vaginal wall, are examined for lacerations. The doctor is called to suture any lacerations found. A sterile pad is placed over the vulva and the soiled bed linen is removed. The patient should now be made comfortable and covered warmly, as many women become cold and shivery after delivery.

Observations after delivery

The mother's temperature, pulse and blood pressure are taken and recorded, and the fundus and vaginal blood loss are again checked. The mother may then be given her baby to cuddle, her reaction to him being noted by those attending her, as it may give some indication of how she is going to accept her child. When the mother has had a few minutes with her baby in her arms, he is tucked down in his cot beside her and both mother and baby are then left to rest quietly for a while. A tray of tea for the patient and her husband is usually very much appreciated at this time.

Examination of the placenta and membranes

Whilst the patient is resting the midwife will examine the placenta and membranes to ensure that they are complete and healthy. If they appear incomplete, the doctor will be informed because there is a risk of haemorrhage occurring if fragments of placenta or membrane are retained in the uterus. The placenta may be weighed and should be approximately one sixth of the baby's weight. Three blood vessels, one vein and two arteries, should be found in the umbilical cord. On occasions when only one artery is present this may be associated with a fetal abnormality. Blood loss is measured and all these findings are recorded in the patient's notes.

Subsequent nursing care

It is important to check repeatedly that the uterus remains contracted and that the lochia are normal, as the most likely time for haemorrhage to occur is within an hour or so of delivery. The mother is given a bedpan and encouraged to pass urine, as a full bladder pre-disposes to a relaxed uterus and heavy blood loss. A vulval wash is then given and sterile pads applied to the vulva.

Finally, the mother will be given a blanket bath, change into a fresh nightdress, clean her teeth and comb her hair.

Care of the baby after delivery

1. Warmth

When the mother has seen her baby for a few moments after delivery, he is transferred to a warm cot. The towel, now damp, in which he was received at birth is removed and he is wrapped warmly, leaving only his face exposed. Babies lose heat very quickly at this time due to evaporation from their wet skin and because the labour ward temperature of $21°$ C is very much cooler than that in utero. The infant is then tucked down on his right side with the head of the cot slightly lowered to encourage further drainage of mucus from the air passages. After a few minutes, if the baby is breathing normally, the cot is raised to the horizontal.

2. Respiration

It is essential to ensure that respiration is established as soon as possible after birth, because hypoxia may result in brain damage. Further mucus extraction is often necessary, and if the baby is not pink and crying after this, oxygen has to be given by face mask. The midwife observes the baby closely while he is in the labour ward to ensure that his colour remains pink and that he has no respiratory difficulties.

3. Apgar score

At one minute after birth the Apgar score is assessed. This is a method of evaluating the baby's condition by observing five vital signs: respiratory effort, heart rate, colour, muscle tone and response to stimuli. A score of 0, 1 or 2 marks is given for each sign and the points are then totalled. An Apgar score of 8–10 indicates that the baby is in good condition at birth. Moderate birth asphyxia is present if the score is between 4

Table 1. Apgar scoring system

Sign	0	1	2
Heart rate	Absent	Slow – below 100	Over 100
Respiratory effort	Absent	Weak cry Gasping	Good cry
Muscle tone	Limp	Some flexion	Well flexed Active
Reflex irritability	No response	Some response Grimace	Good response Cry, Cough
Colour	Blue/Pale	Body pink Extremities blue	Pink

and 7, whereas a score of 3 or less indicates that the baby is severely asphyxiated and requires urgent resuscitation. The Apgar score is assessed again at 5 minutes after birth and repeated at 5-minute intervals if a score of 8–10 has not been achieved. Few babies have an Apgar score of 10 at one or five minutes after birth, because until the peripheral circulation is well established, the extremities remain rather cyanosed.

4. Mother and baby relationship

The importance of the mother seeing and cuddling her baby soon after delivery cannot be overemphasized. She should be given the opportunity to hold her baby and begin to form her very important bond with him as soon as possible. The mother is sometimes a little disappointed in her baby's appearance at birth, especially when he is unwashed, and thus reassurance is often necessary at this time.

5. Identification of the baby

The next essential is to label the baby clearly, otherwise there is a grave risk in a maternity unit of mothers being given the wrong baby. There are various methods of labelling babies, a common one being to write the baby's name and the mother's hospital registration number on two labels which are checked by the mother before being securely fastened round the baby's wrist and ankle.

6. Care of the umbilical cord

Great care must be taken to avoid the introduction of infection; thus the nurse will wash her hands before attending to the cord and use a sterile pack containing the scissors, swabs and a haemostat. The haemostat may be either a rubber band, plastic clamp or nylon tape ligatures and will be applied to the cord about 2·5 cm from the umbilicus. The excess cord is cut off with sterile scissors and the end of the cord dried. An antiseptic such as 1 per cent. chlorhexidine in 70 per cent. spirit is then applied to the cord and the end may be sealed with a plastic dressing spray. It is vital to check the cord frequently for bleeding during the next six hours or so. A blood loss of 30 ml from a baby is equivalent to 600 ml in an adult. Very thick cords are most likely to bleed and thus require especially close observation.

7. Examination of the baby at birth

This examination is carried out soon after birth by the midwife in the mother's presence. Most mothers are anxious to be assured that their baby is normal and like to see him being examined. The midwife unwraps the baby and firstly observes his general appearance. Do his features, for instance, appear normal? She also notes the colour, muscle tone and activity of the baby. Then a systematic examination is carried out from head to foot to detect any congenital abnormality and evidence of birth injury or infection. Most babies are normal and healthy and the midwife will usually be able to reassure the mother that all is well. If an abnormality is found, however, it is recorded in the case notes and the doctor informed. He will examine the baby and explain the situation to the parents.

8. Birth weight and measurements

The baby's birth weight is checked by a second nurse; his length and head circumferences are then measured and all this information recorded in his notes. The mother is usually very eager to know her baby's weight and is told as soon as possible. The baby's temperature is taken rectally, using a low reading thermometer, and he is washed, dressed and wrapped warmly. He can then be given to his mother to hold and, perhaps, breast feed.

9. Breast feeding

If the mother wishes to breast feed, the baby is usually put to the breast in the labour ward soon after delivery. He has a nourishing feed of colostrum, which has a high content of protein, sugar and antibodies. The action of the baby sucking at the breast causes a release of the hormone oxytocin from the posterior pituitary gland and this causes the uterus to contract. This breast feed thus benefits both mother and baby and the mother is very encouraged if her baby feeds well.

If the condition of mother and baby is satisfactory after at least an hour has elapsed since delivery, they will be transferred to a post-natal ward.

7. Normal Puerperium: Physiology and Management

The physiology of the puerperium

The puerperium is the period following the completion of labour during which the reproductive organs return to their non-pregnant state and lactation becomes established. As this process is a physiological one, its duration is subject to variation but lasts for approximately 6 to 8 weeks. Contained within the puerperium is the lying-in period, which is defined by the Central Midwives Board as a period of not less than 10 nor more than 28 days after the birth of a baby during which the continued attendance of a midwife on the mother and infant is required.

Changes in the reproductive organs

The return of the reproductive organs to their non-pregnant state is called involution, when the following changes take place.
1. **The uterus.** The *size* of the uterus decreases from about 15 cm long × 11·5 cm wide × 9 cm deep at the end of labour, near to its original size of 7·5 cm × 5 cm × 2·5 cm.

The *fundal height* of approximately 12·5 cm above the symphysis pubis at the end of labour, decreases to about 7·5 cm by the end of a week, and is non-palpable in 10–12 days.

Its *weight* decreases from 1 000 g to 500 g after seven days and to 60 g in about 6 weeks, but the uterus is probably never quite as small again as before the first pregnancy.

The *placental site* measures approximately 12 cm in diameter at the end of labour, and diminishes gradually to heal completely in about six weeks.

The anterior and posterior uterine walls are in firm apposition following the expulsion of the placenta, but during the next 24 hours this strong contraction eases a little, leaving a cavity which is warm, dark and moist, with the devitalised tissue making it a potential breeding ground for harmful bacteria that may be readily introduced from the exterior via the lax vulva, vagina and cervix. For this reason, the importance of preventing infection during the puerperium cannot be too highly stressed. The *lower uterine segment* again becomes the isthmus of the uterus. The *cervix* is soft and flabby after labour, but gradually regains its tone, admitting one or two fingers by the end of a week, but only a finger tip at 6 weeks, when the external os takes the form of a transverse slit.

The processes involved in involution of the uterus are:

(a) *autolysis*, which means self-destruction, as uterine muscle fibres are broken down by proteolytic enzymes, passed into the circulation and excreted in the urine; and

(b) *ischaemia* (a reduction in blood supply) leading to atrophy of the uterine muscle (myometrium).

The *lochia* are the discharges from the uterus in the puerperium, which have a characteristic, rather unpleasant odour, and are alkaline in reaction. The amount is variable, and is heavier and lasts longer than a normal period, diminishing from the second day, but lasting from ten to fourteen days and sometimes longer. The constituents are blood, decidua, liquor, debris, leucocytes, serum and cervical mucus. Little fresh blood is lost after the third day, although there may be a slight recurrence, especially during breast feeding. However, persistent or heavy blood loss is abnormal.

All the decidua is discharged in the lochia except the basal layer from which the endometrium regenerates.

Menstruation recommences towards the end of the puerperium or during the next month or two, often being delayed in the woman who is breast feeding.

By the end of the puerperium, the uterus is once more a pear-shaped pelvic organ, anteverted and anteflexed with its anterior and posterior walls in apposition. The endometrium has reformed, the myometrium is back to non-pregnant thickness, but the perimetrium probably remains wrinkled.

2. The ovaries and Fallopian tubes return to the pelvic cavity with the uterus. Ovulation recommences before menstruation, so that a woman may become pregnant again before she has a period.

3. The vagina and the vulva regain their tone and their vascularity is reduced. The vaginal rugae reform, and all that remains of the hymen are the fleshy tags known as carunculae myrtiformes.

Changes in other organs

1. The breasts. Following delivery, the circulating oestrogen level falls, causing the anterior lobe of the pituitary gland to release prolactin, and by the third day the milk 'comes in'. The breasts at this time are full, tense and usually tender, but by the fifth or sixth day the tension has reduced considerably; subsequently the lactating breast is fairly firm but comfortable, with increasing fullness as the baby's feeding time becomes due. When a woman is fully breast feeding her baby, her breasts may be only slightly larger than normal.

2. The pelvic floor. The two halves of the levator ani muscles, separated by the descent of the fetus, are gradually restored to their normal position as the muscle fibres regain tone.

Post-natal exercises are necessary to regain adequate support of the uterus and bladder. Incised or torn superficial muscles heal with fibrous tissue formation, and the perineal body regains its shape and muscle tone.

3. The abdominal wall. The rectus abdominis muscles regain their tone assisted by post-natal exercises, but the abdomen may still be lax at the end of the puerperium.

4. The urinary tract. Urinary output increases for two or three days because of autolysis of uterine fibres and a decrease in the volume of plasma and tissue fluid. The ureters return to their normal size and shape and the bladder and urethra regain their position and tone.

5. The alimentary tract. Smooth muscle tone improves in the cardiac sphincter and intestines, resulting in the disappearance of heartburn and a gradual improvement in bowel function.

6. The circulatory system. The volume of blood decreases and the blood regains its usual viscosity, so that the blood pressure returns to normal. Varicosities improve gradually, but following the pressures of labour, varicose veins and haemorrhoids are often more troublesome than usual early in the puerperium.

7. The respiratory system. The basal lobes of the lungs, which are compressed in late pregnancy from the pressure of the rising uterus under the diaphragm, become reventilated.

8. The skeletal system. Pelvic joints and ligaments, which soften in pregnancy and stretch in labour, return to normal in about three months.

9. The endocrine system. The level of oestrogen falls resulting in the release from the anterior pituitary gland of prolactin, which initiates lactation. Thyroid activity is reduced. The pituitary gonadotrophins recommence their cycle and ovulation may well occur during the puerperium, so that a woman can become pregnant before menstruation recurs.

10. The emotions. The patient's emotional state is very much affected by the bodily changes in the puerperium, and mild depression is common following the elation which usually occurs in the first day or two after delivery. A woman may well experience anxiety or inadequacy as she begins to form a relationship with her new baby. The protective maternal instinct is strong, but feelings of love towards the baby may take time to develop and she may have difficulty in adjusting her feelings between the new baby and any other children. The emotions tend to stabilize towards the end of the puerperium.

Management of the puerperium

In normal post-natal care, the midwife plays a major role in helping the woman to recover from pregnancy and labour and assisting her along the road to successful motherhood. This care is frequently given in the woman's own home, following current policy in many obstetric units to discharge patients before the tenth post-natal day.

Whether in hospital or at home the following aspects of management require consideration.

1. Atmosphere

Because of the instability of the emotions after childbirth, a tranquil environment should be aimed at, with minimal stress. Nurses sometimes find this dull after the brisk bustle of many types of nursing, but it is essential for emotional recuperation. The need for privacy, when intimate nursing procedures are being carried out, should be balanced against the need for company at other times. The new mother is very sensitive to the attitudes of her attendants towards herself and her baby, and remarks are often recalled or repeated months or even years later. The attendant, therefore, requires a gentle but positive approach to establish a good rapport, and must be tactful in her advice and comments. Tiredness and depression are relatively common complaints in the months following childbirth, much of which can probably be avoided by good management of the early post-natal period.

2. General health

(a) Rest. Undisturbed sleep should be ensured for the first few nights, by using drugs if necessary, e g nitrazepan (Mogadon) 5–10 mg. Bed rest should be encouraged in the daytime during the early days, with at least one hour spent in the prone or semi-prone position to encourage anteversion of the uterus.

Relations and friends often flock to see the new baby, and his acceptance is important to the mother, but these visits must not be at the expense of her rest. The importance of adequate rest on resumption of household duties should also be stressed.

(b) Exercise should take the form of graduated activity. Early ambulation is important to prevent venous stasis but standing about should be discouraged.

Breathing, leg, abdominal and pelvic floor exercises should be taught and practised daily for at least six weeks after delivery.

(c) Diet. A well-balanced, nourishing diet should be taken. The woman who is breast feeding requires extra protein and fluids and a high-energy intake, but she should be advised not to over-indulge in certain foods, e g fruit, which could cause her baby to have loose stools. Iron supplements help to restore a normal haemoglobin concentration in those who are anaemic or had a heavy blood loss at delivery. Her weight should be near to normal by the end of the puerperium.

3. Observations and recordings

General

Temperature and **pulse rate** should be recorded twice-daily for three days and then daily until the tenth day. A rise in either is a significant finding, suggesting infection or haemorrhage. **Blood pressure** is recorded shortly after delivery and then only if required. **Urinary output** is measured for 24 hours after delivery and a daily record kept of the frequency of **bowel action.**

Specific

The woman should be examined daily for the first ten days of the puerperium in the following way:

(*a*) Note her general appearance and behaviour, and ask about her appetite and how well she sleeps.

(*b*) Examine and record the tension and consistency of her breasts, the milk-flow and the condition of her nipples and areolae.

(*c*) With the woman lying flat on her back and having just passed urine, palpate her abdomen to ensure that she is emptying her bladder adequately and to feel the size and consistency of her uterus. The fundal height above the symphysis pubis may be measured and charted to give an indication of the progress of involution.

(*d*) Examine the lochia on the vulval pad for amount, colour and consistency.

(*e*) Examine the perineum for healing if tearing occurred or an episiotomy was performed at delivery. Non-absorbable sutures, if used, are usually removed on the sixth day.

(*f*) Inspect her legs for oedema and inflammation and ask if she has felt pain in them.

4. Nursing care in the post-natal period

The immediate nursing care after delivery is described in Chapter 6 on normal labour. Following this initial care, little nursing is required by healthy women after normal delivery, now that most are allowed up for toilet purposes within a few hours of having their babies. Much post-natal care is, therefore, directed towards the prevention of complications, e g infection, and the treatment of discomfort.

(a) Prevention of infection. Puerperal infection should be thought of as being almost entirely preventable. Prevention starts at the planning stage of maternity units, and their siting, size, layout and construction must be with this in mind. Post-natal wards need to be light, airy and easy to keep clean. All grades of staff and visitors must, if they are infected, be excluded from the wards, and patients with any type of infection which could endanger others must be isolated. There should be an adequate supply of bed linen so that soiled articles may be replaced immediately, and a high standard of hygiene must be maintained throughout. One of the advantages of early transfer home is a lower risk of cross infection.

(b) Bathing. Following a post-delivery rest of several hours, the woman is accompanied to the bath. The first bath should be supervised as the mother is often a little unsteady from the effort of labour and the change in intra-abdominal pressure. Subsequently, the woman should be encouraged to take a bath at least twice-daily for the first few days when the lochia are heavy and the perineum is healing, and thereafter once a day. A bidet and shower may be used instead of a bath.

(c) The breasts. Most women, whether breast feeding or not, have some breast discomfort. The discomfort starts about the third day and lasts for several days, varying from a feeling of fullness to marked pain and tenderness. During this time the breasts should be supported with a firm binder, carefully applied after each feed or bath, and graduating to the woman's own nursing brassiere as the breasts become more comfortable. Hot-bathing the breasts may ease the tension, and analgesics, e g paracetamol (Panadol) 1 g, are often given. If the breasts are overfull, they should be massaged and enough milk expressed to make them comfortable, but as this procedure stimulates milk production, it must not be done if lactation is being suppressed.

(d) The uterus. Contractions of the uterus continue after labour, but are usually painless. However, they may be painful, particularly if any products of conception or blood clots are retained, for the uterus will contract strongly in an effort to expel them. These painful contractions are more common in multigravidae and are called after-pains. The treatment is to remove the cause: the woman should be asked to empty her bladder, and then an attempt is made to expel any blood clots from the uterus by gentle fundal pressure. Analgesics are often required. Contractions are also sometimes noticed during breast-feeding, and the lochia may be heavier at these times. Reassurance that this is a normal process which aids involution, is all that is required.

(e) The perineum. Frequent bathing will soothe a sore

perineum and reduce the risk of infection. Careful drying of the area, with soft tissues and the frequent changing of soiled vulval pads will promote healing. The use of an ice-pack on a badly bruised perineum lessens the likelihood of oedema, which retards healing and causes pain. It is important to help the woman to find a comfortable position, especially at feeding times, and analgesics may be prescribed to reduce discomfort.

(f) The bowels. If the woman has had an enema or suppositories at the beginning of labour and no food for twelve hours or more, no bowel action should be expected until two or three days after delivery, but from then on normal action should be resumed. However, many women require mild aperients in the post-natal period.

5. Mothercraft and health education

A very important part of the management of the puerperium is the teaching and supervision of mothercraft, including revision of the aspects taught at ante-natal classes. In these days of small families, many women have had little opportunity to handle a new baby before their own comes along, and skills which were once acquired early in life now need to be taught. In addition, most women will have to manage the new baby and the household with only their husbands to help, and without the continual support of other relatives, once supervision by the midwife has ceased. At this time a woman is usually very receptive of advice, and principles of mothercraft and health education may be learned which will lay a good foundation for her family's health.

(a) Hygiene. Because of the risk of infection to the mother and her new baby, high standards of hygiene must be maintained by her attendants and also taught to the woman herself. One must not assume that hospital procedures are sufficient protection or that the woman's home will be a safe environment. Most mothers, even if careless over their own health, are anxious to do their best for their new baby, especially a first one, and this opportunity for establishing the principles of personal hygiene should not be lost. The importance of hand-washing after using the lavatory or handling vulval pads, and before touching the breasts or the baby, must be stressed.

(b) Feeding the baby. The majority of women who are prepared to try breast feeding should succeed if they have skilled help and encouragement. All mothers should be taught how to prepare artificial feeds and care for the equipment so that they are able to cope should the need arise. The woman who is bottle-feeding her baby requires help and supervision in the early days, and needs to learn the importance of giving plenty of time to her baby but not too much food. (See pp. 112–113.)

(c) **Baby care.** Every mother needs time to get to know her new baby and to form a relationship with him, although she will only require revision in caring for the physical needs if she has had a baby before. Rooming-in, where the baby stays all the time in a cot beside his mother's bed, is now practised in many places, but if facilities are not available for this, the necessity for mother and baby to be together as much as possible must be remembered. As well as learning to feed her baby, the mother should be taught, and supervised in, the changing of napkins and bathing and handling her baby. The care of napkins to prevent infection and sore buttocks must also be emphasized.

(d) **Family planning.** Advice on contraception is often given ante-natally, but tactful enquiries should be made to discover whether advice is required and to ensure that the woman knows where to obtain help. An appointment may be made if necessary (see Chapter 13, Family Planning).

6. Follow-up care

On the tenth day of the puerperium the midwife usually ceases to look after the mother and baby, although she may, if necessary, continue post-natal care for four weeks after delivery. During this time the health visitor will visit the home to assess the condition of the mother and baby, and offer any advice required including the times and location of the local Child Health Clinic, where the baby's progress will be followed.

7. The post-natal examination

At the end of the puerperium the mother returns to the hospital where she had her baby, or to her general practitioner, for an examination of her general condition, and to ensure that her reproductive organs have returned to their non-pregnant state.

8. The Newborn Baby

Physiology

Having lived effortlessly in the uterus and come through the ordeal of birth, the newborn baby has to exist independently and adapt to a very different environment. This involves major physiological adjustments at birth which include the establishment of breathing and subsequent changes in circulation, the regulation of body temperature, digestion and absorption of food and development of resistance to infection.

The establishment of respiration. During birth the relative reduction of oxygen and accumulation of carbon dioxide in the blood stream stimulate the respiratory centre in the medulla, but if these changes are excessive or prolonged, the respiratory centre becomes depressed. It is thought that the centre is further stimulated by sensory impulses which result from the compression of the chest wall during delivery, the impact of cold air on the skin and the handling of the baby at birth. The first breath inflates the lungs, and the alveoli then stay inflated because of the presence of a lining liquid called surfactant, which has the special property of keeping the alveoli from collapsing by being able to change the surface tension of the alveoli according to the pressure in the lungs. The newborn baby's respirations are irregular, mainly abdominal, and rapid at about 40 per minute.

Changes in the circulation. When the baby starts to breathe at birth and the umbilical cord is cut, major circulatory changes take place to enable him to obtain oxygen via his lungs (see p. 43).

Temperature control. Having been used to a constant environmental temperature of 37·7°C in utero, the newborn infant has to adjust to a cooler atmosphere of about 21°C. His heat-regulating mechanism is inefficient at birth and, as it adjusts to a changed environment, tends to cause an unstable body temperature. The newborn baby has stores of brown fat, however, which can rapidly be utilized for heat production when required in the early days of life. After delivery his temperature quickly falls in the cooler atmosphere, especially as he is wet and losing heat by evaporation. To prevent excessive heat loss from his relatively large surface area, the infant must be quickly dried, wrapped in warm blankets and placed in a heated cot, and, to prevent hypothermia, he must subsequently be nursed in a warm atmosphere without prolonged exposure.

Digestion. Independent existence requires the newborn infant to suck, swallow, digest, absorb and excrete for himself. The breast fed baby takes colostrum (see p. 90) initially which is very easily digested and highly nourishing, but cow's milk, even if specially prepared for human infants, is more difficult to digest. During the first two days the baby passes a sticky, greenish-black stool called meconium, which has gradually accumulated in the bowel from about the 16th week of intra-uterine life, and consists of mucus, epithelial cells, swallowed amniotic fluid, bile pigments and fatty acids.

Kidneys. From mid-pregnancy the fetus has passed urine into the amniotic sac. He may pass urine during or immediately after birth, which should be noted, and further micturition should occur within 24 hours. The amount of urine passed gradually increases during the first week of life as the fluid intake rises, but as the kidneys are immature at birth, excretion of substances such as sodium is inefficient.

Blood. The fetus has a high haemoglobin level of 170–200 g/litre (17–20 g per 100 ml) of blood, but after birth, when he obtains his oxygen directly from the lungs, this amount is no longer necessary and thus excess red blood cells are broken down. The resultant release of bilirubin may cause neonatal jaundice (see p. 123).

The low prothrombin level in the newborn may result in a deficient blood clotting process; thus vitamin K, 0·5–1 mg, may be given intra-muscularly to babies at birth to increase their production of prothrombin. It is especially necessary for those infants most likely to bleed, namely pre-term babies, those with abnormal or excessive moulding, or those who have had an operative or traumatic delivery.

Weight. During the first three to five days of life the baby may lose up to 10 per cent. of his birth weight but should regain it by the 10th–12th day. This is due to loss of tissue fluid, the passage of meconium and a deficient fluid intake, but the baby will subsequently gain about 200–250 g per week.

Reaction to infection. The newborn infant is particularly susceptible to infection because he has been protected from the common organisms whilst in the uterus and thus, when exposed to them for the first time after birth, he has little resistance because his immunity is not fully developed. His immunity to common micro-organisms such as staphylococci, Escherichia coli and proteus will gradually increase over the next few months and years, but during these vulnerable early days and weeks of life, every effort must be made to protect him from infection by reducing the number of organisms in his environment.

The infant, however, will have acquired a passive immunity to some infectious *diseases*, such as measles, because if the mother has had the disease or been immunized, she will have developed antibodies and these are transferred to the fetus across the placenta during the later weeks of pregnancy. These antibodies give the baby a passive immunity for about six months.

Examination of the newborn

A normal baby is born after a gestation lasting between 37 and 42 weeks, his average birth weight being 3–4 kg and length 50–52 cm. Average head circumferences at birth are: sub-occipito-bregmatic 33 cm; occipito-frontal 35 cm.

The midwife makes the preliminary examination of the baby soon after birth and this is followed by a doctor's examination within the next few days. The baby is undressed and examined gently in a warm, well-lit room, preferably in the mother's presence.

General appearance. The infant should have a healthy pink colour, good muscle tone and be vigorous and active. Vernix caseosa, a white, greasy substance, will be found mainly in the skin folds of mature babies but it may cover the trunk of pre-term infants. It is secreted by the fetal sebaceous glands and protects the skin during intra-uterine life. After term, vernix caseosa decreases in amount and thus post-mature babies, having lost this protective covering, tend to have dry, peeling skins.

Lanugo, fine, downy body hair, though mainly a feature of

pre-term infants, is often still present on mature babies in the first few weeks of life.

Head. The size and shape of the baby's head are noted and the presence of moulding and a caput succedaneum (see p. 179). Sutures and fontanelles are gently traced with the finger and the size observed. Occasionally, a baby develops a swelling on his head called a cephalhaematoma a few hours after birth (see p. 179).

Face. Any unusual appearance is observed, for this can indicate abnormality as in, for example, the mongoloid features characteristic of Down's syndrome (see p. 180). The upper border of the ears should be level with the eyes, low set ears being associated with abnormal conditions. Normal racial features must be taken into consideration, for example at birth, the eyes are always grey/blue in Caucasians (white races), but may change colour during the first year. It is about six weeks before a baby's eyes begin to focus properly, although momentary fixing may be observed at feed times from about a week old. Many babies have wandering eye movements during these early weeks, but these are of no significance. No tears are produced when crying for the first month or so, thus the baby is particularly susceptible to eye infections at this time. A conjunctival haemorrhage is sometimes present at birth, caused by pressure during delivery, but it is absorbed within two to three weeks.

Tiny white spots called milia are sometimes present over the nose, due to blocked sebaceous glands. So called 'stork marks' may also be apparent just above the bridge of the nose, on the nape of the neck and sometimes on the upper eyelids; these are capillary naevi and fade during the first or second year.

Many babies develop sucking blisters, which do not contain fluid, in the midline of the upper lip. The mouth should be examined in a good light for a cleft palate; small, white spots, called Epstein's pearls, may be seen at the junction of the hard and soft palate. Sometimes a tongue-tie is present, when the frenulum is attached almost to the tip of the tongue, but no treatment is usually necessary. Very occasionally, the baby is born with one or two teeth which tend to be loose and are, therefore, easily extractable.

Trunk. The neck is examined for any swelling or undue webbing and the chest observed for respiratory movements.

The doctor auscultates the heart and lungs. Some babies develop enlarged breasts in the early neonatal period, due to withdrawal of maternal oestrogens from the baby's blood; no treatment is necessary, unless there is evidence of infection, because the condition subsides spontaneously. Secretion of colostrum may also occur; it is often called 'witch's milk' and must not be expressed because this would bruise the tissues, which may then become infected and cause mastitis. The abdomen protrudes slightly in the newborn; the umbilical cord should be examined, noting especially the number of vessels in the cord.

External genitalia. The labia of a baby girl are gently parted to note the urethral and vaginal orifices. A thick, white vaginal discharge is often present after birth and vaginal bleeding, known as pseudo-menstruation, may occur as a result of oestrogen withdrawal. The baby boy's penis is examined to note the position of the urethral orifice; no attempt should be made to retract the foreskin as it is adherent to the glans penis and separates spontaneously during the early years of life. Both testes should be palpable in the scrotum in mature male babies.

Limbs. The limbs are examined to note equal length, normal movements and the presence of deformities, such as talipes (club foot). The hip joints are examined for congenital dislocation of the hips (see Barlow's test, p. 105). Fingers and toes should be counted and any webbing noted.

Back. The baby is then turned over and his back inspected. By running a finger down the spine abnormalities of the vertebral column may be detected. A baby of Eastern or negroid ancestry may have a blue patch, rather like a big bruise, usually over the sacral area, which is known as a Mongolian blue spot. The presence of a sacro-coccygeal dimple should be noted because there is sometimes a blind sinus, though it is rarely of serious significance, and, finally, the anus is examined for patency, usually by attempting to insert a rectal thermometer.

Reflexes

The doctor will carry out a neurological examination of the baby, because certain stimuli evoke specific responses which give some indication of normal neuro-muscular development.

The **sucking reflex** is tested by introducing a finger or teat into the mouth when vigorous sucking should occur.

The **rooting reflex** is most apparent when the baby is hungry. A touch on the cheek or corner of the mouth results in the baby turning to the side stimulated to search for food. Pressure in the palm of the hand or sole of the foot results in the **grasp reflex**. The infant may grasp the examiner's hand so tightly that, when traction is applied, he can be lifted up.

The **Moro reflex** is elicited when the baby is startled. If the head and trunk are supported on the examiner's arm and hand and the head suddenly allowed to fall a few centimetres, the infant responds by adbucting, then extending his arms with his hands open, but his fingers often remain curved; this is followed by adduction of the arms as in an embrace. When held upright with his feet on a firm surface, the infant attempts to straighten his trunk and make alternate stepping movements, thus demonstrating the **walking reflex**.

Screening tests

Various tests are carried out on all babies in the early neonatal period to detect the presence of certain conditions.

A **meconium test,** for the diagnosis of cystic fibrosis, is carried out on the first specimen of meconium passed. In a positive result the protein content of meconium will be high because the pancreatic enzymes necessary for the digestion of protein are absent. The result is thick, viscid meconium which may cause obstruction of the small intestine.

The **Guthrie test** is performed between the sixth and the fourteenth day for the diagnosis of phenylketonuria. Capillary blood from a heel prick is collected and sent to the laboratory; a positive result occurs when there is a high level of the amino-acid, phenylalanine, due to a deficiency of the enzyme necessary for phenylalanine metabolism. Further tests will be made if the Guthrie test is positive, because excess phenylalanine leads to cerebral damage.

Barlow's test is carried out for the diagnosis of congenital dislocation of the hips, and is performed by the midwife in her examination of the baby at birth and subsequently by the doctor. With the baby lying on his back, the examiner holds each leg with knees and hips flexed. The middle fingers are placed over the greater trochanters and the thumbs on the inner aspects of the thighs. With the baby's hips partly abducted, the examiner applies upward and inward pressure with his fingers, followed by downward and outward pressure with his thumbs to try and move the head of the femur in and out of the acetabulum. A click will be felt if the head of the femur slips in or out of the acetabulum. A baby with unstable hips should be re-examined a few days later and, if the instability persists, referred to an orthopaedic specialist.

Management of the newborn

Warmth. The surrounding temperature should be 21–24°C, both by day and night. Babies should be warmly, but not tightly, wrapped as they need freedom of movement. To detect hypothermia, the rectal temperature is recorded for the first few days with a low-reading thermometer; it should not fall below 36°C.

Hygiene. It is common practice to wash only the face, hands, buttocks and groins for the first few days, because, when bathed, a baby tends to become chilled and is more likely to sustain skin abrasions which could become infected. The mother is usually shown how to bath her baby on about the sixth day, and subsequently baths him daily, under supervision. The main points the mother should be taught are to ensure that the room is warm and to avoid prolonged exposure of her baby. Before removing the baby from his cot, she should prepare the equipment and place it within easy reach, including clean clothes, towel and the baby's own supply of soap or special cleansing liquid, cotton wool, petroleum jelly and dusting powder. A sterile gallipot of water and sterile swabs are necessary for the baby's face, and a spirit preparation and antiseptic powder for the cord. Containers for the soiled linen and swabs are required, and, finally, the bath water is prepared at a temperature of 38°C. The baby is undressed, apart from his napkin, and wrapped in a warm towel. When the mother has washed her own hands she gently washes his face, avoiding the eyes, and dries it with sterile swabs. Having tested the temperature of the bath water, the baby's hair is washed and dried. The napkin is next removed, the buttocks cleaned and the baby either soaped all over and rinsed in the bath, or immersed in the bath containing the special cleansing liquid which is not rinsed off, and gently dried. After treating the umbilicus, petroleum jelly is applied to the buttocks and the baby is warmly dressed. During the daily wash or bath the baby should be carefully examined for any signs of infection.

It is also important to teach the mother that the baby's buttocks should be washed with soap and water or special cleansing liquid, dried carefully, and a barrier cream applied each time she changes the napkin, otherwise bacteria on the skin convert urea in the urine to ammonia and the buttocks become sore due to an ammonial burn.

Cord Care. The cord is treated once or twice daily with an antiseptic preparation, such as 1 per cent. Chlorhexidine in 70 per cent. spirit, and an antiseptic powder. To aid early separation the cord may be treated with a spirit preparation each time the napkin is changed. The cord separates by a process of dry gangrene on about the fifth day, but treatment continues until the umbilicus is healed.

Stools. Newborn infants normally pass meconium within 24 hours of birth, often several times. As meconium tends to stick to the skin, it is important to apply petroleum jelly to the buttocks to aid in its removal. A brownish-green stool, known as a changing stool, gradually replaces meconium by the second or third day, and by the fourth or fifth day, the baby's stools are yellow. A breast-fed baby passes a soft, bright yellow, inoffensive stool, whereas an artificially fed baby has a paler, firmer stool with a slightly offensive odour.

Prevention of infection. It is vital to protect the newborn baby from infection because he has little resistance to organisms, and thus an apparently mild infection can rapidly become a serious condition. A baby who succumbs to any infection is immediately isolated to prevent cross-infection. The infant is colonized (invaded) by micro-organisms after birth and great care should be taken to keep the skin intact, thus preventing the entry of bacteria. Antiseptic preparations are used for cleaning the skin and the cord, the latter being especially susceptible to infection.

Micro-organisms in the environment can be reduced by good ventilation, thorough daily cleaning and the avoidance of dust. Rooming-in, whereby the baby remains beside the mother's bed, helps to prevent cross-infection, as fewer people handle the baby. Cots should be well spaced and each baby must have his own equipment kept in an attached container. All attendants should be free from infection, and conscientious hand-washing before and after handling each baby is essential.

The promotion of breast feeding helps to reduce the incidence of neonatal infections, because breast-fed babies receive positive protection from the antibodies in human milk. Breast milk is also sterile, whereas great care must be taken in the preparation of artificial feeds to avoid the introduction of organisms.

Crying. At first there may be a tendency to think that crying is always an expression of hunger, but the baby also cries because he is too hot or too cold, in pain, thirsty, uncomfortable or perhaps feels lonely and wants mothering. Crying is his only means of communication and his mother will gradually learn to interpret her baby's cry and thus understand his needs.

The mother/baby relationship. The baby should be handled by his mother as soon as possible after birth. The bond established from the very beginning of life is strengthened by handling, as mother and baby, and father too, grow to know one another. Rooming-in helps to promote this close bond because the mother has more contact with her baby. She should be encouraged to talk to him and she will soon find that he shows signs of response, thus deepening their relationship.

Feeding

Breast feeding

During pregnancy, the mother supplies all her baby's nutritional requirements from the nutrients in her blood. If she breast feeds, she continues to supply her baby with nourishment from her own body.

Comparison of breast and artificial feeding

For most mothers and babies breast feeding is undoubtedly the best and most enjoyable method of feeding and also fosters a very satisfactory interdependent relationship. Baby dependence develops, of course, when the mother bottle feeds her baby, but it is not such an intimate experience and the mother, perhaps, does not handle her baby so much because other people may also feed him, and she does not depend on her baby for comfort and relief at feed times. Because breast milk is the perfect food for the infant, whereas cows' milk has to be adapted to simulate human milk as much as possible, the problems of hypernatraemia and hypocalcaemia (see pp. 112 & 122) which may occur in artificially fed babies do not occur in those who are breast fed.

It may take several weeks for breast feeding to become fully established, but the mother will then find it is easier and entails less work. Some mothers worry because they do not know how much the baby is taking from the breast, whereas they can see exactly how much milk is consumed from a bottle. A mother should be reassured that she will soon learn to judge whether her baby is satisfied or not.

Breast-fed babies develop fewer infections in the first year of life, partly because contamination of human milk is unlikely, but also because the baby receives some positive protection from the antibodies present in breast milk. In addition, the large intestine of the breast-fed baby has a higher acidity and different bacterial flora which are thought to increase his resistance to gastro-enteritis.

Obesity in infancy is mainly a problem of artificially-fed babies. Breast-fed babies are less likely to grow fat and this is also true of the mother who breast feeds. The fat cells are laid down in the first year or two of life and thus, if the baby becomes fat, he will always have a tendency to obesity, which may lead to the development of hypertension and cardiovascular disease in later life.

A few women are unable to breast feed because of severe debilitating or infective conditions, such as tuberculosis. Breast feeding may be inadvisable if the mother is taking certain drugs, which will pass in her milk to the baby, and babies with rare disorders, such as lactose intolerance, may not be able to take breast milk. Occasionally, a baby will have a congenital malformation, such as cleft lip and palate, which makes breast feeding difficult, but the mother could express her milk and give it to the baby by spoon, or by bottle using a special teat.

Management of breast feeding

Attitudes have an important influence on the success of breast feeding, favourable attitudes on the part of the mother, her husband and the staff being more likely to promote success. Many authorities employ a lactation sister who is responsible for the promotion and supervision of breast feeding. Careful ante-natal assessment will highlight the problems which may occur and steps can thus be taken, where possible, to avoid them. If sore nipples or overfilling, for instance, are particularly likely to occur, the patient may be given 3 doses of ethinyl oestradiol 0·02–0·04 mg, commenced within 12–24 hours of delivery, to delay the production of milk. This not only reduces the likelihood of overfilling, but also the risk of sore nipples, as the baby can be introduced more gradually to breast feeding.

The mother who breast feeds needs sufficient rest and a good diet to enable her to meet the dietary requirements of her infant without jeopardizing her own health.

Preparation of mother and baby for feeding

After washing her hands and breasts, the mother should sit comfortably and have clean tissues and a watch or clock within easy reach. A sore perineum sometimes makes sitting upright difficult and the mother may then prefer to lie on her side to feed her baby.

The baby's napkin is changed and any discharge from his eyes or nose removed to reduce the risk of the mother developing a breast infection. The baby needs to be fully awake to feed successfully and, unless he is crying, the mother should take a few minutes to admire and talk to him before starting the feed.

Supervision of feeds

Feeding times should be quiet, unhurried and relaxed periods which both mother and baby enjoy. Most mothers need help for the first few days, so the midwife should be present to supervise feeds until she can confidently manage alone. She should be taught to fix her baby on the breast by holding his head in the crook of her arm with his mouth near to her nipple. The baby usually opens his mouth in response to the touch of the nipple on his lips, thus demonstrating the rooting reflex. It is important that the baby grasps both the nipple and the areola in his mouth, because the ampullae, the small, milk containing reservoirs, lie beneath the areolae. The breast must be kept away from the baby's nose whilst he is sucking to allow him to breathe freely. After the feed the baby is gently removed from the breast to avoid damage to the mother's nipple.

Feeds are usually limited to two minutes only at each breast until the third or fourth day after delivery, when the breasts fill. Thereafter the time is increased by about two minutes daily until the baby is feeding for 10 minutes each side. The baby may be fed at regular three- or four-hourly intervals or on demand, the demand-fed baby being fed when he wakes, rather than at specified times.

The mother is taught to start the feed on alternate breasts each time, because the baby sucks more vigorously at the beginning of the feed when he is hungry and will probably nearly empty the first breast, and tends to take less milk from the second.

Complementary feeds. The baby is sometimes given a bottle feed in addition to being breast fed for the first three to four days, until the mother produces sufficient milk to satisfy him.

Supplementary feeds. A supplementary feed is a bottle feed which is given in place of a breast feed.

Test weighing is only carried out if it is really necessary to find out how much milk the baby is taking from the breast. The baby is weighed before and after being breast fed, wearing exactly the same garments, and the difference between the two weights gives some indication of the amount of milk taken. Test weighing should be carried out for 24 hours, and if the baby is being underfed complementary feeds are given; if he is overfed, the time at the breast is reduced.

Artificial feeding

As yet, no exact replica of human milk has been developed and, therefore, cows' milk has to be modified for babies.

Table 2. Constituents of Milk

	Colostrum	Human milk	Cows' milk
Protein	8·0%	1·5%	3·5%
Carbohydrate	3·5%	7·0%	4·5%
Fat	2·5%	3·5%	3·5%
Minerals	0·4%	0·2%	0·75%
Water	85·6%	87·8%	87·75%

Comparison of human milk and cows' milk

The protein in human milk is two parts of lactalbumen to one part of caseinogen, whereas in cows' milk the protein is nearly all caseinogen, which is less easily digested by babies. Because the carbohydrate content of the cows' milk is less than that of human milk, sugar is added to supply the additional joules (calories). The amount of fat is about the same, but the fat globules in cows' milk are bigger and more indigestible. The high mineral content of cows' milk is of particular concern because it increases the solute load (see glossary) presented to the kidneys. Healthy babies can usually cope with this, provided feeds are made up correctly using the right proportion of milk to water, but if the feeds are too concentrated or if the baby becomes dehydrated in hot weather or due to an infection, the high mineral content can be dangerous. The newborn kidneys cannot cope with the excretion of the excess sodium load and thus hypernatraemia, which is a raised concentration of sodium in the blood, develops and may cause permanent brain damage.

Cows' milk is adapted for babies, therefore, by diluting it with water, which reduces the high protein and mineral levels and dilutes the fat content; sugar is added to raise the carbohydrate level. Most manufacturers now produce a modified dried milk with a particularly low mineral content for infant feeding, and this should be recommended where breast feeding is not possible.

Types of milk

Dried milk. The milk is dried by spraying it into hot air, or pouring it onto hot rollers. To reconstitute the milk, the manufacturers' instructions must be followed explicitly. It is essential that the milk powder is accurately measured in the scoop provided for that brand of milk, and mixed in the correct quantity of boiled water; this minimizes the risk of hypernatraemia, especially if a modified milk is being used.

Vitamins A, C and D are added to dried milk preparations, and many manufacturers also add iron.

Evaporated milk has about two thirds of the water removed by heating, and the concentrated milk is then canned. To reconstitute and dilute it for infant feeding, it is usual to start feeds with one part of evaporated milk and two parts of boiled water and to add sugar. Evaporated milk is not recommended for infant feeding, however, because of its high mineral content.

Fresh cows' milk is not recommended for infant feeding either, except in an emergency, when it must be boiled, diluted with boiled water and have sugar added. The casein is not so well broken up by boiling as by drying methods and, again, the mineral content is high.

Calculation of feeds

A baby will require approximately 150–170 ml per kg by the time he is about a week old, and thereafter until mixed feeding is introduced at the age of four to six months. Small feeds are given during the first few days, the amount being gradually increased until the baby is having his full requirements. Feeds may be calculated as follows:

Per kg body weight in 24 hours

1st day	60 ml	
2nd day	60 ml	Amount divided
3rd day	90 ml	into 5 or 6
4th day	120 ml	feeds in 24 hours
5th day	150 ml	

Although it is sometimes necessary to increase the feed from 150 to the maximum of 170 ml per kg to satisfy a very hungry baby, it is important to avoid overfeeding. A crying baby will often settle if he is given boiled water to quench his thirst between feeds.

The baby's first feed is usually a clear fluid such as dextrose 5 per cent., and should be given within three to four hours of birth; thereafter, he should have milk feeds every three or four hours or on demand.

Sterilization of equipment

Sterile, pre-packed feeds in disposable bottles and with disposable teats are widely used in hospitals today. However, the mother must be taught how to sterilize feeding equipment and make up feeds and ideally she should practise so that she can do it efficiently at home. It is vital she should understand that hygienic preparation of feeds and careful sterilization of feeding equipment is necessary to reduce the risk of her baby developing gastro-enteritis.

Plastic or glass wide-necked, upright bottles are easy to clean and the feed can be made up in the bottle, thus reducing the risk of contamination. After use the bottles should be rinsed in cold water, washed thoroughly in warm, soapy water with a bottle brush, rinsed well and then sterilized either by boiling for five minutes or, more commonly, by total immersion in a 1 in 80 solution of sodium hypochlorite for one and a half hours. Teats are rinsed and cleaned with salt before being washed and sterilized with the bottles. A fresh solution of sodium hypochlorite should be made up daily.

9. Neonatal Complications
Low Birth-weight Babies

Low birth-weight babies

One of the aims of good obstetric care is to reduce the number of low birth-weight babies born, because of the higher mortality and morbidity rates associated with these small infants. Low birth-weight babies are of two kinds:

1. **Pre-term infants** who are born before the 37th week of pregnancy and thus, being immature, are not ready to adapt to extra-uterine life.
2. **Light-for-dates infants** who are small for their gestational age due to intra-uterine malnutrition. Infants who are below the 10th percentile (see glossary) for their gestational age are considered to be light for dates. Mean weight is approximately the 50th percentile (see Fig. 21).

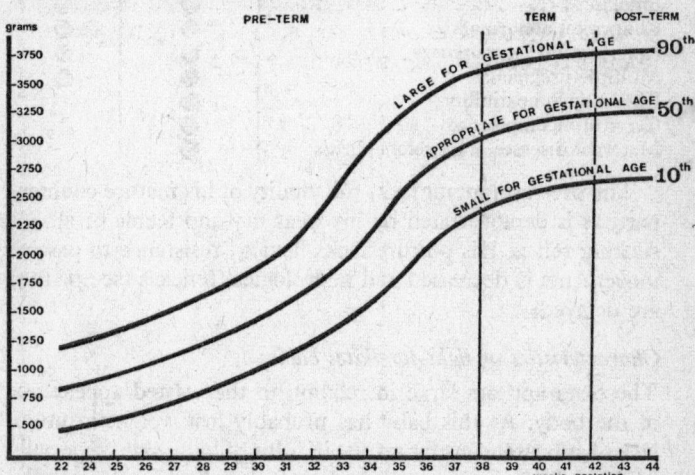

Fig. 21. Centile chart to show expected weight for gestational age.

Some babies, of course, are both pre-term and light-for-dates.

Characteristics of pre-term babies

The shorter the gestational age, the more marked are the characteristics. The infant has a large, soft head with wide sutures and fontanelles, a small chest and a protruding abdomen. Lack of subcutaneous fat results in a red skin and prominent surface veins. Lanugo may be apparent on the face and trunk and the nails tend to be soft, as are the ears, which fold easily due to lack of cartilage. In baby girls the labia minora are not covered by the labia majora and in boys the testicles are usually incompletely descended. The weight of the pre-term infant is variable, though usually 2 500 g or below, whereas length, being less than 47 cm, is a more reliable feature of prematurity.

Table 3. The main causes of low birth-weight infants

	Pre-term	Light-for-dates
Pre-eclampsia and eclampsia	●	●
Placental insufficiency	●	●
Smoking	●	●
Congenital abnormalities	●	●
Ante-partum haemorrhage	●	●
Multiple pregnancy	●	●
Rhesus incompatibility	●	
Cervical incompetence	●	
Maternal diseases, e g pyelonephritis	●	

The pre-term infant lacks the vitality of his mature counterpart, as is demonstrated by his weak cry and feeble or absent sucking reflex. His posture lacks flexion, resistance to passive movements is decreased and neurological reflexes (see p. 104) are delayed.

Characteristics of light-for-dates babies

The head appears large in relation to the wasted appearance of the body. As this baby has probably lost weight in utero, lack of subcutaneous fat results in folds of loose skin, especially in the axillae, groins, neck and abdomen. In severe cases the baby may look wizened and old and have a dry, peeling skin, perhaps discoloured by meconium. The abdomen is often hollowed and the cord thin, flabby and, perhaps, meconium-stained. Muscle tone is variable, the baby usually being active and showing signs of hunger, unless suffering from prolonged intra-uterine hypoxia. Neurological responses usually correspond to gestational age.

Problems of low birth-weight babies

Most complications occur with pre-term babies, because they are immature and not ready to adapt to extra-uterine life, but some are common to both pre-term and light-for-dates infants.

Table 4. Common complications with low birth-weight babies

	Pre-term	*Light-for-dates*
Birth asphyxia	●	●
Hypoglycaemia	●	●
Hypocalcaemia	●	●
Respiratory distress syndrome	●	Meconium inhalation (see p. 128)
Cerebral haemorrhage	●	
Jaundice	●	
Anaemia	●	
Infection	●	

Management of low birth-weight babies

At birth. The baby should be skillfully delivered, following an episiotomy, in a hospital which has a special-care baby nursery. Resuscitation of the baby at birth is carried out by a paediatrician and, when the mother has seen her baby, he is then transferred to the special-care nursery.

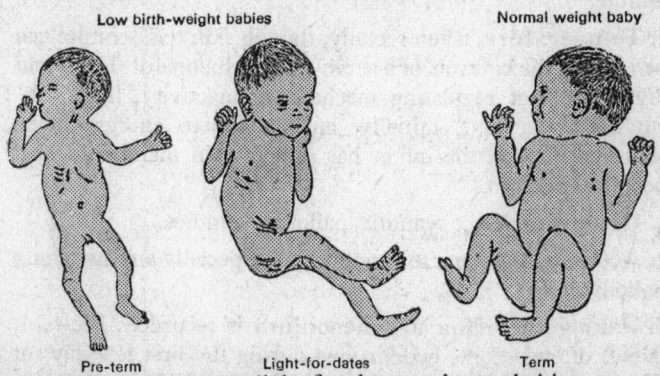

Fig. 22. Pre-term, light-for-dates and term babies.

Subsequent care. The baby is usually nursed in an incubator at a temperature of 32–35°C because temperature control is very unstable in small babies and adequate warmth is essential. Servo-control of incubator temperature is an advantage, as it automatically changes according to the infant's skin temperature and thus helps to maintain his body temperature at 36–37°C; humidity of about 60 per cent. is usually satisfactory. Oxygen is given, when necessary, to prevent cyanosis, but the concentration of oxygen must always be carefully monitored, either by an oxygen analyzer which measures oxygen content in the incubator, or more accurately, by checking the infant's arterial oxygen levels. Too much oxygen may result in retrolental fibroplasia, in which changes in the retinal vessels and peripheral separation of the retina occur; fibrosis, opacity behind the lens and blindness ensue. The condition is unlikely to occur if the incubator oxygen level is kept below 30–40 per cent. and the pO_2 (tension of oxygen in the blood) below 16 kPa (120 mm Hg).

Observations

The following functions must be observed and recorded.

1. **Respirations,** especially signs of respiratory distress syndrome (see p. 121). Very small or ill babies will be nursed on an apnoea mattress which sounds an alarm if the baby stops breathing for a specified time.

2. **Apex beat,** which should range between 120–160 beats per minute.

3. **Temperature,** taken rectally, though skin temperature can be read on the controls of a servo-control incubator. Due to an immature heat regulating mechanism, inactivity, little subcutaneous fat and, initially, an inadequate energy intake (calorific intake), the infant has difficulty in maintaining his body temperature.

4. **Colour,** to detect cyanosis, pallor or jaundice.

5. **Activity** and **muscle tone,** noting especially any twitching or convulsions.

6. **Passage of urine** and **meconium** is recorded. Pre-term babies often become oedematous during the first few days of life due to relatively poor renal function. They may also

develop abdominal distension, usually due to constipation, which, if severe, may cause respiratory difficulties.

7. **Screening for hypoglycaemia** is carried out at three- to four-hourly intervals for the first 72 hours, using Destrostix paper strips.

Nursing care

Minimal handling and maximal observation are essential principles in the care of low birth-weight infants. The baby is turned regularly and necessary cleansing is carried out gently in the incubator. Every effort is made to avoid infection, as pre-term babies are especially susceptible and react badly; handwashing before and after attending to the baby, the wearing of individual gowns for each infant and the use of the baby's own equipment are all essential precautions. It is particularly important that no staff with any infection should care for these small infants.

Feeding

The method of feeding depends on the size, maturity and condition of the baby. Very small, immature babies or those who are ill may initially be fed intravenously, but this is gradually replaced by continuous or intermittent milk feeds via an indwelling naso-gastric tube. Bottle or breast feeds are started when the baby is ready to suck. Early feeding is advocated to prevent hypoglycaemia, the first feed of dextrose being given within two hours of birth. Milk feeds are then started, breast milk being preferable, if available. On the first day of life the baby is given 60 ml per kg body weight, and this is increased daily by 30 ml per kg, until the baby is having 180–200 ml per kg by the 5th or 6th day. The feeds may be further increased up to 300 ml per kg, if well tolerated, for very small babies, i e those under 1 500 g. Small, frequent feeds are advisable because the cardiac sphincter is poorly developed, and thus if the stomach is overdistended regurgitation and inhalation may occur, especially as the cough reflex is poorly developed or absent in pre-term babies.

A preparation containing vitamins A, B, C and D is started when the baby is a week old and iron therapy at about one month. Pre-term babies become anaemic due to inadequate iron stores and delayed production of red blood cells by the bone marrow, and so regular haemoglobin estimations and iron therapy are essential.

Mother/baby relationship

It is important that the mother should have as much contact with her child as possible, especially in the early days, as separation at this stage can later adversely affect her mothering ability. The parents should be welcomed into the special care nursery, be allowed to touch their baby in his incubator and encouraged to handle and learn to care for him as soon as possible. Before the baby is discharged from hospital, the mother is usually admitted into a mother/baby unit where she learns to care for her baby by day and by night.

The paediatrician usually follows up low birth-weight infants after discharge from hospital to assess their progress and development.

Birth asphyxia

Birth asphyxia occurs when the baby fails to breathe at birth, although a heartbeat is present. Moderate birth asphyxia is present if the Apgar score is between four and seven, whereas a score of one to three indicates severe asphyxia. The cause may be a blocked airway, an immature or damaged respiratory centre or one which has been depressed by drugs, or it may occur as a result of intra-uterine hypoxia.

Management

1. The air passages are cleared.
2. The baby is dried, wrapped warmly and placed in a resuscitation cot with head lowered.
3. Oxygen is given by mask by intermittent positive pressure.
4. The baby is stimulated, often by flicking his feet.
5. If the mother has had pethidine or morphine derivatives, which depress the respiratory centre, within two to three hours of delivery, the baby is given an antidote such as nalorphine (Lethidrone) 0·5–1 mg intramuscularly or intravenously.
6. If the baby does not respond to these measures or is severely asphyxiated, medical aid is summoned immediately and the baby intubated.

7. Subsequently the baby who has been severely asphyxiated is nursed in the special care nursery where he will be carefully observed for a few days and will be followed up after discharge from hospital.

Respiratory distress syndrome

In this condition increasing respiratory difficulty occurs, usually within six hours of birth. It affects pre-term infants, especially those of less than 35 weeks gestation, babies born by Caesarean section and the baby of the diabetic mother. Recent work suggests that the incidence of this condition in preterm babies can be reduced by giving the mother dexamethazone 4 mg 8-hourly by intra-muscular injection for 72 hours before delivery. Dexamethazone increases the production of surfactant (see p. 100) in the fetal lungs and thus reduces the incidence of the syndrome.

Signs of respiratory distress syndrome (RDS)

1. A progressive rise in the respiratory rate: it often exceeds 100 per minute.
2. An expiratory grunt.
3. Marked sternal and intercostal recession.
4. Cyanosis.

There is both respiratory acidosis due to carbon dioxide retention and metabolic acidosis due to chronic hypoxia, which causes the blood pH to fall. In addition, the high carbon dioxide level exerts a depressant effect on the respiratory centre and may cause apnoeic attacks.

Management. The infant is nursed in an incubator in high humidity and with sufficient oxygen to prevent cyanosis. In severe RDS, high concentrations of oxygen may be necessary and thus the arterial pO_2 should be monitored regularly and maintained at the optimum level of 9–12 kPa (70–90 mm Hg), to avoid both anoxic brain damage and retrolental fibroplasia.

An intravenous infusion of 10 per cent. dextrose (50 g in 500 ml) is set up, to which sodium bicarbonate is added to correct the metabolic acidosis. Frequent estimations of blood gases are necessary and the amount of sodium bicarbonate is adjusted accordingly.

Minimal handling is carried out until the baby shows signs of improvement, usually 48–72 hours after the onset of the condition, but during this time he is under constant observation, and blood glucose levels are monitored to detect hypoglycaemia. When the signs of improvement become evident, milk feeds via a naso-gastric tube can be started. If, however, the condition deteriorates, the prognosis is poor; many such babies die from intraventricular haemorrhage caused by hypoxia. Mechanical ventilation may be employed for some babies with severe RDS.

Hypoglycaemia

Hypoglycaemia occurs when the blood glucose level falls below 1·1 mmol/litre (20 mg per 100 ml), usually within 72 hours of birth. It affects mainly low birth-weight babies who have inadequate stores of glycogen, and the babies of diabetic mothers, but other predisposing causes are birth asphyxia, respiratory distress syndrome and hypothermia.

Signs of hypoglycaemia are twitching leading to convulsions, lethargy, hypotonia, shallow respirations and apnoeic attacks.

Prevention is by feeding soon after birth and by screening all babies at risk using the Dextrostix strip-tests. If these tests indicate hypoglycaemia, blood specimens are sent to the laboratory for more accurate blood glucose estimations.

Management. Immediate treatment is necessary to prevent brain damage and thus the baby may be given 2 ml of 50 per cent. dextrose (1 g in 2 ml) either orally or intravenously, depending on the severity of the condition, followed by frequent milk feeds, or, if the condition is severe, an intravenous infusion of dextrose 10 per cent. (50 g in 500 ml).

The baby should be followed up after discharge for assessment of neurological function.

Hypocalcaemia

Hypocalcaemia, or neonatal tetany, occurs in some artificially-fed babies between the fifth and eighth day of life, if the blood calcium falls below 1·9 mmol/litre (7·5 mg per 100 ml). The high phosphorous content of cows' milk causes a rise in blood phosphate which cannot be excreted rapidly enough by the immature kidneys and the calcium level therefore falls in a seesaw manner. Neonatal tetany is apparent as irritability, followed by twitching and, sometimes, repeated convulsions. The treatment is to give calcium, usually orally with feeds, although in severe cases it may be given intravenously. Recent work has shown that hypocalcaemia adversely affects the dentine of the teeth, thus predisposing to caries.

Jaundice

The main causes of jaundice in the neonatal period are:
1. physiological jaundice, due to immaturity of the liver;
2. haemolytic disease, due to Rhesus or ABO incompatibility;
3. infections such as umbilical sepsis, pyelonephritis, septicaemia, or virus infections causing hepatitis and liver cell damage; and
4. congenital malformations; rare conditions, such as obliteration of the bile duct which is invariably fatal.

Physiological jaundice

The high red blood cell count of 6–7 million per mm^3 (cu mm) of blood required in utero is no longer necessary after birth when the baby obtains oxygen via his lungs; thus the excess red blood cells are broken down and fat-soluble or unconjugated bilirubin passes into the blood stream. This has to be converted into water-soluble or conjugated bilirubin by an enzyme in the liver before it can be excreted. In many babies, especially those who are immature, this enzyme is deficient or absent and thus there is delay in conjugation and the circulating fat-soluble bilirubin causes yellow staining of the skin. Physiological jaundice usually appears on the second or third day, reaches a peak by the fifth or sixth day and then gradually fades.

Treatment. The serum bilirubin is monitored until the level begins to fall. The baby is given extra fluids to dilute the serum bilirubin, and phototherapy with ultraviolet light which decomposes the bilirubin in the skin into non-toxic, water-soluble substances ready for excretion. In the rare event of the serum bilirubin approaching 342 micromols/litre (20 mg per 100 ml), an exchange transfusion would be necessary to prevent the development of kernicterus and subsequent brain damage.

Rhesus incompatibility

About 85 per cent. of Europeans have the D antigen in their red blood cells and are thus Rhesus positive, the remaining 15 per cent. being Rhesus negative. The Rhesus factor is inherited genetically, one gene coming from each parent.

For Rhesus incompatibility to occur, the mother must be Rhesus negative, which is described as dd (i e she does not have the D gene) and the father Rhesus positive. He may be homozygous, that is DD, when all his children will inherit the Rhesus factor (D), or heterozygous, Dd, when some of his children will inherit the positive gene (D) and some the negative (d). D is the dominant gene.

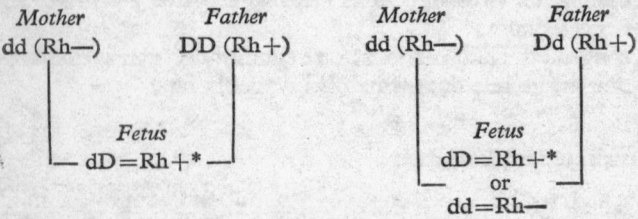

* Rhesus incompatibility: a potential hazard.

However, Rhesus incompatibility occurs only in about 15 to 20 per cent. of cases when a Rhesus negative mother bears a Rhesus positive child. In these cases where there must be a flaw in the normal placental barrier, sufficient fetal Rhesus positive blood passes into the maternal circulation to stimulate the mother to produce antibodies. These antibodies in turn may cross the placenta and break down the fetal red blood cells, thus causing anaemia. Severe haemolysis of red cells and consequent anaemia may lead to cardiac failure and marked oedema, a condition known as hydrops fetalis when the fetus is usually stillborn.

The most likely time for fetal blood to enter the maternal circulation is during the third stage of labour, thus Rhesus incompatibility rarely complicates the first pregnancy unless there is some placental separation, or the placenta becomes a particularly ineffective barrier towards the end of pregnancy. Rarely today has a Rhesus negative mother developed antibodies following the wrongful administration of Rhesus positive blood, because the Rhesus factor has been recognized since the early 1940's.

Prevention of rhesus incompatibility

The Kleihauer test is carried out on a maternal blood sample soon after delivery to estimate the number of fetal cells which have passed into the maternal circulation during the third stage of labour. All Rhesus negative women who have delivered a Rhesus positive baby are given an intramuscular injection of Anti D Immunoglobulin within 72 hours of delivery, to destroy the fetal cells and thus prevent the formation of antibodies which could affect future pregnancies. With these measures the incidence of Rhesus incompatibility has fallen markedly over the last few years.

Diagnosis of Rhesus incompatibility

All ante-natal patients have their A B O and Rhesus group determined early in pregnancy and their blood is examined for the presence of antibodies. Rhesus negative patients have repeat antibody tests at monthly intervals from the 26th week of pregnancy, more often if antibodies are detected. An abdominal amniocentesis (withdrawal of amniotic fluid with syringe and needle) is also carried out if antibodies are found, to examine the liquor for bilirubin content because a high level indicates excessive breakdown of fetal red blood cells.

Management of Rhesus disease

During pregnancy. In severe cases of haemolytic disease before the 32nd week of pregnancy, the fetus may be given an intra-peritoneal blood transfusion to prolong life until premature induction of labour will be less hazardous. Labour may be induced, when necessary, after the 34th week.

After delivery. Cord blood specimens are obtained immediately after delivery and sent to the laboratory for the following investigations: (1) Blood group; (2) Rhesus factor; (3) Serum bilirubin; (4) Haemoglobin; and (5) Coombs' test, which is positive if maternal antibodies are detected on the fetal red cells. If the Coombs' test is positive, cord blood haemoglobin is below 148 g/litre (14·8 g per 100 ml) and bilirubin above 60 micromols per litre (3·5 mg per 100 ml), the baby is likely to become jaundiced within 24 hours of birth, and an exchange transfusion may be necessary.

An exchange transfusion is carried out to avoid the danger of kernicterus by removing blood containing maternal antibodies and bilirubin from the baby's circulation and replacing it with fresh Rhesus negative blood. Sometimes two or three exchange transfusions may be necessary, though this occurs less frequently nowadays as the infant is also treated by phototherapy.

Follow-up of any child who has suffered from severe jaundice is necessary to observe developmental progress and to treat anaemia.

Neonatal infections

Signs of infection tend to be rather non-specific in the newborn and are:

1. temperature: may be normal, raised or, commonly, subnormal
2. colour: pale/grey or jaundiced
3. frequent vomiting
4. drowsy and lethargic or may be fretful
5. reluctance to feed
6. failure to gain weight
7. anxious expression
8. convulsions may occur

The **principles of treatment** are:

1. isolation of the baby;
2. examination by a doctor;
3. appropriate swabs and specimens are collected and sent to the laboratory for culture and sensitivity; any baby who fails to thrive is fully screened for infection by taking nose, throat and umbilical swabs, and three urine and stool specimens; the doctor may request a blood culture and, if he suspects meningitis, perform a lumbar puncture;
4. local treatment;
5. systemic treatment, as necessary.

Note that only the local and systemic treatment will be described for the following conditions, as the first three principles are common to all.

Skin infections. (Usually staphylococcal.)

(a) Pustules may occur singly or in crops, mainly in warm, moist skin folds. They should be swabbed with an antiseptic lotion (local treatment) and, if they multiply, treated with an antibiotic (systemic treatment).

(b) Paronychia is a nail-bed infection usually caused by the baby sucking his fingers and damaging the skin. Treatment is the local application of an antiseptic solution and the baby should wear mittens.

(c) Sore buttocks may become infected or occur as a result of an infection such as thrush. The buttocks are gently cleaned with an antiseptic solution and exposed to the air. Heat treatment aids healing and the appropriate treatment is given for the cause of the infection.

(d) Pemphigus neonatorum is a very serious skin condition characterized by watery blisters. It is highly contagious and thus strict isolation is essential to prevent an epidemic.

Eye infections

A slight, sticky discharge from one, or possibly both, eyes may occur in the early neonatal period and is only rarely associated with bacterial infection. It usually responds quickly to cleansing with normal saline.

Ophthalmia neonatorum is a purulent discharge from the eyes of the newborn, commencing within 21 days of birth. It is a notifiable condition, commonly caused by the staphylococcus aureus, although it can also be caused by streptococci or Escherichia coli and, occasionally, by the gonococcus, in which case it is a particularly serious infection which may result in blindness.

Prevention starts by treating maternal infections in the antenatal period and by gently cleaning the eyes at birth. Subsequently it is best to avoid touching the eyes, unless there is a discharge which indicates infection, when the eyes should be irrigated with normal saline, and, if prescribed by the doctor, eye ointment applied. The baby is nursed on the affected side to prevent the discharge infecting the other eye. An antibiotic will be necessary if the infection is severe.

Umbilical infections

Umbilical infections, caused mainly by the staphylococcus

aureus and Escherichia coli, are characterized by a moist, offensive cord, perhaps peri-umbilical inflammation and delay in cord separation. The cord is treated four-hourly with an antiseptic solution, and an antibiotic is usually prescribed because umbilical infections may lead to thrombophlebitis of the umbilical vein, hepatitis or septicaemia.

Infections of the alimentary tract

Thrush is characterized by white patches in the mouth which cannot be removed. It is caused by the fungus Monilia (Candida) albicans, and may spread throughout the alimentary tract. Treatment with oral Nystatin 100 000 units six-hourly for four to seven days is effective.

Gastro-enteritis is an extremely serious and highly infectious condition, the causative organism usually being the pathogenic Escherichia coli, one of the Salmonella group or, less commonly, a virus. The first sign is often reluctance to feed, followed by vomiting and frequent, loose, watery, yellow/green stools. Strict isolation is vital, preferably away from the maternity department. Intravenous therapy to treat dehydration and correction of electrolyte imbalance are essential.

Urinary tract infection. Any baby who fails to thrive should be screened for a urinary tract infection, because pyelonephritis is not uncommon in the neonatal period. A specimen of urine is collected either by fitting an adhesive polythene bag over the genitalia or, if a sterile specimen is required, by suprapubic aspiration, when urine is withdrawn from the bladder with a syringe and needle inserted just above the symphysis pubis. If pus cells and bacteria are found in the urine, the baby is treated with the appropriate antibiotic, often for three to six weeks. The urine is then re-examined to ensure that the infection has cleared. Follow-up is necessary as the infection may recur and could be associated with a congenital abnormality of the urinary tract; thus, intravenous pyelography may be required.

Respiratory tract infection

This very serious condition in newborn infants may be due to aspiration of infected or meconium-stained liquor during delivery, or the inhalation of milk or vomit later. The infant is nursed in an incubator and given humidified oxygen to relieve cyanosis, and the appropriate antibiotic is administered.

Meningitis

Associated with septicaemia, the additional signs are a bulging anterior fontanelle and, perhaps, neck rigidity and convulsions. The diagnosis is confirmed by lumbar puncture, and treatment with antibiotics and anticonvulsants is started immediately.

10. The Complications of Pregnancy

Minor disorders of pregnancy

The minor disorders of pregnancy often cause patients much discomfort and occasionally develop into more serious conditions.

Vomiting may occur from about the fourth to the fourteenth week of pregnancy. The cause is not fully understood, but it could be hormonal in origin, perhaps due to the high levels of chorionic gonadotrophin circulating at this time, or for dietetic, metabolic or psychogenic reasons.

Treatment. Vomiting commonly occurs in the early morning and the patient is therefore advised to rise slowly, having had a drink and dry biscuit in bed. Small, frequent, easily digestible meals should be taken during the day and a milky drink at night. Drugs should only be taken if prescribed by a doctor, because of their possible harmful effect on the developing fetus. Excessive vomiting occurs occasionally and the condition deteriorates into hyperemesis gravidarum, when the patient becomes dehydrated and ketotic and requires hospital admission and treatment.

Frequency of micturition may occur throughout pregnancy but is particularly troublesome during the first trimester, when the enlarging uterus is in the pelvis, and again after the 36th week when the presenting part becomes engaged. There is, unfortunately, no remedy for this trying disorder.

Constipation occurs because progesterone relaxes plain muscle and thus diminishes peristaltic action. It should be treated, where possible, by increasing fluid and roughage intake, but in some cases a mild aperient such as Senokot may be necessary.

Heartburn is also caused by the relaxing effect of progesterone, this time on the cardiac sphincter, when acid stomach contents reflux into the oesophagus causing a burning sensation. As pregnancy advances the condition worsens because the stomach is displaced by the enlarging uterus.

Treatment. Small frequent, easily digestible meals and sleeping in a semi-recumbent position at night help to relieve heartburn. Antacids may be prescribed.

Varicose veins may develop or, if already present, become worse in pregnancy due to the relaxation of plain muscle in the veins and impaired venous return. They are most commonly found in the legs but may also occur in the rectum (haemorrhoids) or vulva.

Treatment. Elastic tights should be worn but must be put on before rising each morning to prevent the veins over-filling with blood. The patient is also advised to avoid long periods of standing and to sit with her legs raised.

Haemorrhoids are treated with an ointment or suppositories, such as Anusol, and constipation must be avoided. Vulval varicose veins are supported with a firm pad during pregnancy, and the patient is delivered in hospital because of the risk that they may rupture and cause haemorrhage during delivery.

Cramp commonly occurs in the legs at night and may be due to ischaemia of the leg muscles which is often relieved when the patient sleeps with the foot of the bed raised. An adequate intake of vitamin B, calcium and salt is required, as the cramp could be due to a deficiency of these substances.

Backache is common, especially towards the end of pregnancy when the pelvic joints relax, but it may also be associated with poor posture, pyelonephritis or the onset of labour.

Vaginal discharge. An increased leucorrhoea (normal vaginal discharge) occurs in pregnancy, but infective conditions may also develop.

Monilial vaginitis is caused by a fungus, Monilia (Candida) albicans, which results in a white, curdy discharge, intense irritation and soreness. A vaginal swab is taken to confirm the diagnosis, extra care with hygiene is necessary and Nystatin pessaries should be prescribed for 7–10 days.

Trichomonad vaginitis is characterized by a frothy, profuse, offensive discharge, which again causes severe irritation. The treatment is metronidazole (Flagyl) 250 mg daily by mouth for 10 days for both the woman and her husband.

Gonorrhoea is a very serious infection which attacks the mucous membrane of the cervix and urethra; it gives rise to a purulent vaginal and urethral discharge with frequency and pain micturition. If the disease is untreated, the baby's eyes infected during delivery which could result in corneal damage and blindness.

Major disorders of pregnancy

Pre-eclampsia

Pre-eclampsia is a condition peculiar to pregnancy which occurs usually after the 28th week and is characterized by three cardinal signs, a raised blood pressure, oedema and proteinuria. A diagnosis of pre-eclampsia is made if the patient has any two of these three signs. If untreated, it may progress to eclampsia when fits occur and the woman's life and that of her fetus are endangered.

The cause of pre-eclampsia is unknown but it most commonly affects primigravidae, especially the very young, and women over 35 years of age, obese patients, those with a multiple pregnancy or hydatidiform mole (early onset), or women suffering from diabetes, hypertension or renal disease. The patient usually feels well until eclampsia is imminent, thus early detection of signs at the ante-natal clinic is essential.

Diagnosis

Hypertension in pregnancy is considered to be 130/90 mm Hg or above, but a rise in diastolic blood pressure of 10–15 mm Hg or more above the level recorded in the early weeks of pregnancy is always of significance.

Oedema occurs in the feet and ankles, hands, the face and finally becomes generalized. Excess weight-gain may also be indicative of abnormal fluid retention.

Proteinuria is usually the last sign to appear and is always serious. A midstream specimen of urine must be obtained to exclude contaminants such as vaginal discharges, and sent for laboratory examination to differentiate between urinary tract infection and hypertensive proteinuria.

Management of pre-eclampsia

Hospital admission is necessary and, if the period of gestation is 38 weeks or more, labour is usually induced as the condition will subside within 72 hours of delivery. When pre-eclampsia develops earlier, however, conservative treatment is carried out to allow the pregnancy to continue to as near 38 weeks as possible. This involves:

bed rest which improves the placental circulation and helps to lower the blood pressure;

sedation: amylobarbitone, 100 mg thrice daily, is often prescribed by the doctor;

diet is usually low salt, low carbohydrate and of high biological value (protein).

Essential observations and tests include:
- blood pressure
- presence of oedema
- weight
- daily urinalysis for proteinuria
- fluid intake and output
- abdominal examination, noting especially the growth of the fetus and the fetal heart sounds.

Certain investigations are carried out to assess fetal growth and placental function, because a raised blood pressure causes arteriolar spasm and results in a diminished blood supply to the placenta and thereby less oxygen and nutrients to the fetus.

(a) *Cephalometry* is a reliable method of monitoring fetal growth, when the biparietal diameter of the fetal head is measured by ultra-sound, often twice weekly where the facilities for this procedure are available.

(b) *Measurement of the placental hormones*, mainly *oestriol* and *human placental lactogen*, give some indication of placental function. Oestriol is excreted in the mother's urine and the level can be assessed from a 24-hour collection of urine. A series of oestriol estimations are necessary because, although oestriol excretion should rise progressively to about 60–235 micromols in 24 hours at term, there is a wide variation in daily output. Human placental lactogen is estimated from a sample of the mother's blood and should again rise progressively to between 105–250 nmols/litre serum daily at term. Falling oestriol or human placental lactogen levels suggest failing placental function.

Subsequent management

If the condition improves, increasing activity is permitted and the patient may be discharged from hospital, though more intensive ante-natal care would be necessary as the condition is likely to recur. Rest and observation in hospital continue if there is no improvement and early delivery would then be considered. Occasionally the condition deteriorates markedly and for the first time the patient begins to feel ill as the *signs and symptoms of imminent eclampsia become evident.*

These are:
blood pressure ⎫
oedema   ⎬ all rise markedly
proteinuria   ⎭
severe frontal headache due to cerebral oedema
visual disturbances, mainly flashes in front of the eyes and dimness of vision due to retinal oedema
vomiting due to pressure on the medulla
epigastric pain caused by hepatic haemorrhages
oliguria and, perhaps, haematuria

Management of imminent eclampsia

Effective sedation must be given immediately to try to avert an eclamptic fit and lower the blood pressure, and then labour is usually induced or the pregnancy terminated by a Caesarean section. If this situation arises before 34 weeks, the doctor may try conservative treatment with complete bed rest and sedative, hypotensive and diuretic drugs, often administered intravenously, in an attempt to delay the need for delivery until the fetus is a little more mature, but the risks of eclampsia, placental insufficiency and abruption, and intra-uterine death may outweigh those of prematurity.

Eclampsia

Eclampsia is characterized by convulsions which may occur before or during labour and up to 72 hours after birth.
Dangers of eclampsia. The maternal mortality with eclampsia is about 5 per cent. and the more fits the woman has the greater the risk to her life. Causes of death are asphyxia or pneumonia following inhalation of blood or vomitus during a fit, pulmonary oedema, cerebral haemorrhage, cardiac failure, liver failure or anuria due to renal necrosis. The perinatal

mortality is particularly high, the fetus often dying in utero from anoxia or, following delivery, from immaturity.

Eclamptic fits are similar to epileptic fits and have four phases:

The *premonitory stage*, recognized by facial twitching, followed by the *tonic stage* of intense muscular contractions, during which the patient stops breathing and becomes cyanosed; the *clonic stage* of violent muscular movement follows, the patient froths at the mouth and may bite her tongue; she then lapses into a *coma* which may last for minutes or hours.

Management

During a fit a protective gag is inserted into the patient's mouth and she is turned on to her side and protected from injuring herself; suction is used to clear the airways and oxygen is given until her colour becomes pink.

Subsequent management. The main aims are to prevent further fits and to control the blood pressure, and these are achieved by immediate intramuscular or intravenous injection of sedative drugs, followed by an intravenous infusion of solutions to which drugs such as diazepan (Valium) or a combination of chlorpromazine, promethazine and pethidine have been added. In addition, hypotensive drugs and diuretics may be administered, and antibiotics to prevent pulmonary infection. Any disturbance may precipitate another fit, thus the patient must be nursed in a quiet, single room under constant observation and initially only essential nursing procedures such as turning the patient, mouth care and treatment of pressure areas should be carried out. Vital observations include temperature, pulse, respirations, blood pressure, urinary output (via indwelling catheter) and fetal heart rate. Any restlessness or twitching might herald another fit and signs of labour must be detected by the nurse, as it can progress to an advanced stage without being recognized by the heavily sedated or comatosed patient. The woman is, however, often delivered by Caesarian section.

Care in labour. In addition to the nursing care and observations described, adequate analgesia is essential and can be successfully achieved by epidural anaesthesia. Continuous monitoring of the fetal heart and contractions should be carried out, where possible, and when the patient reaches the second stage the doctor will perform an elective episiotomy and forceps delivery.

After delivery the woman may still continue to have fits for up to 72 hours, so the heavy sedation and care already described will need to be continued.

Bleeding in pregnancy

Any bleeding from the genital tract in pregnancy is abnormal. Bleeding before the 28th week is referred to as bleeding in early pregnancy, whereas after the 28th week, when the fetus is viable, it is called ante-partum haemorrhage.

Bleeding in early pregnancy

The main causes are:

Implantation bleeding which sometimes occurs when the fertilized ovum embeds in the decidua. This is very often confused with a menstrual period.

Abortion, which most commonly occurs in the first 13 weeks of pregnancy.

Ectopic pregnancy when the fertilized ovum embeds outside the uterus, usually in the Fallopian tube. The tube will distend and eventually rupture causing severe pain and haemorrhage, usually between the 6th and 10th weeks.

Hydatidiform mole is a rare cause of bleeding in which there is abnormal development of the chorionic villi, the fetus dies and is absorbed and the villi become cystic and distended until they may resemble a bunch of grapes. The patient complains of vomiting, may develop early pre-eclampsia and on palpation the uterus is often large-for-dates, has a soft, doughy consistency and there are no fetal signs of pregnancy. The diagnosis is confirmed by ultra-sound or, because excessive chorionic gonadotrophin is produced in this condition, a strongly positive pregnancy test in very dilute urine.

Treatment is to empty, or possibly remove, the uterus and the patient is followed up for at least two years, as a malignant condition called chorion carcinoma may develop.

Cervical lesions such as a polyp, erosion or carcinoma may cause bleeding at any time in pregnancy, as may severe vaginitis due to a trichomonal infection.

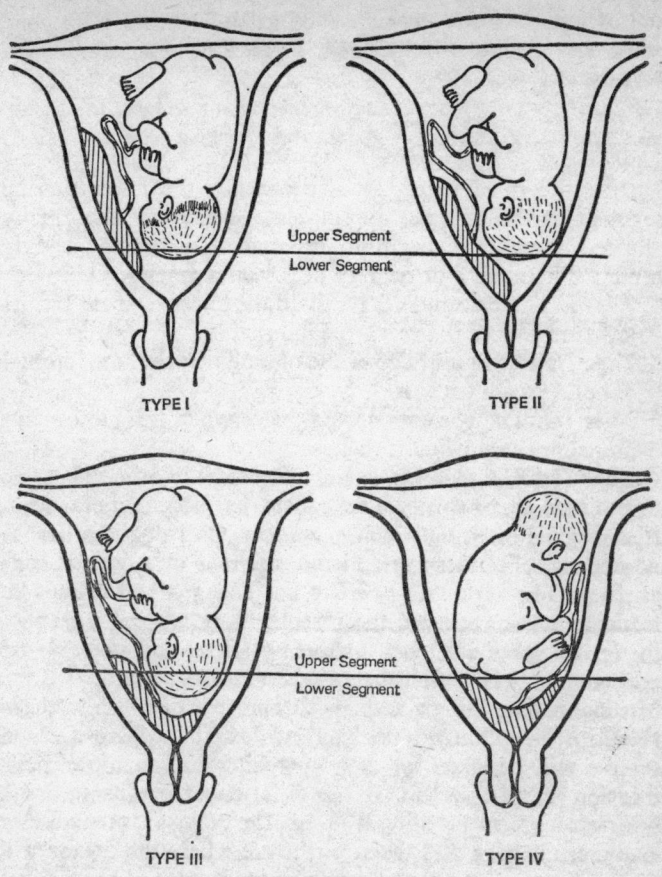

Fig. 23. Placenta praevia.

Ante-partum haemorrhage

Ante-partum haemorrhage is defined as bleeding from the genital tract after the 28th week of pregnancy and before the birth of the baby. There are two main types of haemorrhage: **placenta praevia**, bleeding due to the premature separation of a placenta situated partly or wholly in the lower uterine segment, and

abruptio placentae, bleeding due to the premature separa-

tion of a placenta situated in the upper uterine segment.
Incidental bleeding due to other causes, often cervical lesions, may occur (see p. 136).

Placenta praevia

During the third trimester of pregnancy the lower uterine segment stretches and the placenta which is abnormally situated there may begin to separate and hence bleeding occurs. There are four degrees of placenta praevia.

Type I. The placenta lies partly in the lower segment but its lower edge does not reach the internal os.

Type II. The lower edge of the placenta reaches the internal os but does not cover it.

Type III. The placenta covers the os when it is closed, but not completely when it dilates.

Type IV. The placenta is situated centrally over the os.

Signs and symptoms. The patient has painless, effortless, fresh vaginal bleeding which may recur. On palpation there is no abdominal tenderness and the uterus is of a normal consistency. The presenting part is not engaged and cannot be made to engage because the placenta is occupying the space in the pelvic cavity; thus malpresentations and unstable lie are common. The fetal heart sounds are usually heard.

Management: All patients with ante-partum haemorrhage should be admitted immediately to hospital, where a blood sample will be taken for cross-matching and an intravenous infusion may be set up. If the duration of pregnancy is 38 weeks or more, or bleeding is severe, the patient is prepared for Caesarean section and taken to theatre where the doctor will make an examination per vaginam under general anaesthetic to diagnose placenta praevia. If the placenta is in the lower uterine segment, this examination may cause further placental separation and severe haemorrhage, and an immediate Caesarean section would then be necessary, whereas if no placental tissue is felt or a Type I placenta praevia is diagnosed, vaginal delivery is possible and the membranes are ruptured to induce labour.

In cases of slight to moderate bleeding under 38 weeks gestation, conservative treatment aims to continue the pregnancy until the 38th week to avoid prematurity. The patient is kept quiet, reassured and remains in bed until bleeding has stopped for at least 48 hours. All vulval pads are saved to estimate blood loss and NO examinations per vaginam are made unless the patient is in theatre, for the reason given above.

When bleeding has ceased, investigations are carried out to diagnose the cause of bleeding.

1. *Speculum examination* will show any cervical lesions which could cause bleeding.
2. *Placental localization* is carried out to determine the site of the placenta, the methods being:

   ultrasonic examination;

   soft tissue X-ray;

   radio-active isotopes which are injected intravenously and the uterus scanned with a Geiger counter; the area showing the highest count indicates the placental site; and

   arteriography, when a radio-opaque substance is injected into the abdominal aorta via the femoral artery. Careful positioning of the catheter ensures that both the ovarian and uterine arteries which supply the uterus are filled and the placental site can then be located by X-ray.

If placenta praevia is confirmed, the patient must remain in hospital until delivery as she may at any time have a severe haemorrhage. At 38 weeks, or before if heavy bleeding occurs, an examination under anaesthetic is carried out in theatre, as already described, and the patient is delivered.

Prognosis. With appropriate care both mother and baby should survive in good health, but where immediate hospital treatment is not available, the mortality and morbidity rates for mother and child are greatly increased.

Abruptio Placentae

The cause of abruptio placentae is obscure, though it is associated with high multiparity, pre-eclampsia and trauma. The haemorrhage may be:

   revealed, when all blood lost escapes through the vagina;

   concealed, if blood-loss is retained within the uterus; and

   mixed, when some haemorrhage is concealed and some revealed.

Signs and symptoms of revealed or mixed ante-partum haemorrhage. There may be signs of pre-eclampsia or a history of trauma. On abdominal examination there is usually some tenderness or pain, the uterus may feel tense and, if blood is being retained in the uterus, the abdominal girth increases in size and the patient's clinical condition will be worse than expected in relation to the revealed haemorrhage. Blood loss may be stale if there is some delay in its expulsion.

Management. As the differential diagnosis between abruptio placentae and placenta praevia is not always apparent the initial management is the same. When bleeding has ceased and the examination for placental localization has confirmed that the placenta is in the upper uterine segment, the patient may be discharged home if she is otherwise well, though more intensive ante-natal care than usual will be necessary.

Concealed Abruptio Placentae.

Severe cases are uncommon but exceedingly dangerous as the patient becomes extremely shocked and may die and the fetus is unlikely to survive. Severe, continuous abdominal pain is present due to the retro-placental blood which distends the uterus; abdominal palpation is usually impossible as the uterus is so hard. The patient has all the clinical signs of shock and the fetal heart sounds are rarely heard.

Management. The aim is to restore blood loss and deliver the patient with the least delay. As soon as the patient has been adequately transfused with blood, delivery is expedited, either by surgical induction (see p. 154) and oxytocic infusion or by Caesarean section, if this can be immediately and safely undertaken and a live baby can be expected.

The large retro-placental clot which forms behind the placenta may cause the plasma fibrinogen levels to fall (hypofibrinogenaemia) and this could result in a defective bloodclotting mechanism and post-partum haemorrhage. To avoid such a disaster, plasma fibrinogen levels are checked before delivery and. if low, the doctor may prescribe intravenous fibrinogen.

Prognosis. If there is delay in resuscitating the mother, perhaps because the haemorrhage began at home, her life will be at risk and the fetus will almost certainly die. Prompt resuscitative measures will improve the outlook for both mother and fetus.

Placental insufficiency

In this condition the placenta is not functioning efficiently and consequently fails to transport sufficient nutrients and, perhaps oxygen, to the fetus. Recognition of placental insufficiency is essential because the brain will be damaged if it does not receive sufficient glucose and oxygen, especially after the 37th week when it undergoes a growth spurt. In cases of very severe placental insufficiency the fetus may die.

Causes. Although placental insufficiency is mainly associated with smoking in pregnancy, ante-partum haemorrhage and hypertensive and renal conditions, in many instances there is no known cause.

Recognition. The condition is suspected if the woman fails to gain, or loses, weight in pregnancy and, on abdominal palpation, when the fetus feels small-for-dates.

Management. It is very important to try to ascertain the accuracy of the date of the woman's last menstrual period, as wrong dates may explain why the fetus is small. If the reason is thought to be placental insufficiency, however, the patient is admitted to hospital for rest and observation; the placental blood flow is greatly increased when the woman is resting, hence the fetus receives more food and oxygen. Maternal weight and fetal growth are carefully observed and tests are carried out to monitor placental function (see p. 133). Labour is usually induced at 38 weeks, though earlier delivery may be necessary in severe cases. Fetal distress is a common complication of labour, hence careful fetal heart monitoring is essential (see p. 115 for light-for-dates babies).

Multiple pregnancy

In Western countries twins occur in about 1 pregnancy in 80, triplets 1 in 8 000 and quadruplets in 1 in 500 000. Twins may be uniovular or binovular.

Uniovular twins, commonly known as identical twins, arise from the division of a single fertilized ovum and the fetuses are thus of the same sex, share one placenta and one chorion but each has his own amniotic sac.

Binovular twins are more common, especially among families with a history of twins, and arise from the fertilization of two ova released at the same time. Each fetus has its own placenta,

amnion and chorion and the sex may be the same or different.
Diagnosis. The uterus is large-for-dates and hydramnios may be present. On palpation three 'poles' and a number of fetal parts may be detected. A fetus has two poles, a head and breech; if more than two poles are felt there must be more than one fetus. Two fetal hearts are of little diagnostic value unless the rates are very different when auscultated at exactly the same time. The diagnosis is confirmed by X-ray or ultrasound.
Complications of multiple pregnancy. The minor discomforts of pregnancy are exaggerated, especially pressure symptoms such as varicose veins and dyspnoea, and discomfort may be further aggravated by hydramnios. The incidence of pre-eclampsia and anaemia is increased, and labour often starts prematurely.
Management of multiple pregnancy. Extra rest, a good diet and iron therapy are essential. A period of rest in hospital during the third trimester of pregnancy may be necessary to reduce the risk of premature labour and the possible development of pre-eclampsia.
Complications and management of labour in multiple pregnancy. Both fetuses are usually cephalic presentations, but malpresentations, especially breech, commonly occur, and occasionally the lie of one, or possibly both, fetus is found to be transverse. Cord prolapse may occur, especially after the birth of the first baby when the pelvis is empty and the membranes of the second twin rupture. In the third stage of labour, the incidence of post-partum haemorrhage is greatly increased due to a large placental site and overstretched uterine muscles.
Management. The first stage of labour is conducted normally but an obstetrician, a paediatrician and an anaesthetist should be present at the second stage. The first baby is delivered, resuscitated, labelled Twin I and shown to his mother. The uterine end of the cord must be clamped immediately and an examination per abdomen made to diagnose the lie of the second twin, as it may have changed during the delivery of the first baby. The lie is corrected to longitudinal by external version if necessary, and the fetal heart and maternal pulse and blood pressure are recorded. An examination per vaginam is made to confirm the presentation, to rupture the membranes of the second twin and detect possible cord prolapse. The

mother is encouraged to push with her contractions and the second baby is then delivered. Intravenous ergometrine 0·5 mg is given with the birth of the second twin to reduce the risk of post-partum haemorrhage and the placenta and membranes are delivered by controlled cord traction on both cords together. If the babies are of the same sex and there appears to be only one placenta, the membranes are examined carefully to detect the number of chorions; one chorion suggests uniovular twins, two that they are binovular.

After delivery the mother is closely observed, noting especially the vaginal loss and the condition of the fundus, because she has a tendency to bleed. She is shown her babies and then left to rest.

Polyhydramnios

At term the normal amount of liquor is about 1 000 ml but excessive liquor (polyhydramnios) occurs with uniovular twins, fetal abnormalities, hydrops fetalis (see p. 124) and maternal diabetes.

Acute hydramnios is rare and the onset rapid at about 20 weeks. It usually results in spontaneous abortion.

Chronic hydramnios is more common and develops slowly after the 30th week. On abdominal examination the skin is stretched, taut and shiny, the uterus is large-for-dates, fetal parts are difficult to palpate and the fetal heart is muffled. A fluid thrill can be obtained by flicking one side of the abdomen and feeling the wave of fluid transmitted to the other side. X-ray or ultrasound may help to diagnose the cause of polyhydramnios. The patient usually complains of pressure symptoms such as breathlessness and oedema, and requires hospital admission and rest; if the fetus is abnormal, premature labour may be induced. Complications such as cord prolapse, malpresentations and postpartum haemorrhage may occur in labour.

Medical disorders complicating pregnancy

Anaemia

Causes. Anaemia is common in pregnancy due to the haemodilution which occurs and also because the mother supplies her fetus with iron. Secondary causes of anaemia are bleeding, infections such as pyelonephritis, hookworm infestation, and malabsorption of iron as occurs in achlorhydria. Patients with sickle cell disease or thalassaemia are particularly likely to become anaemic because the abnormal red blood cells are easily haemolyzed (see Glossary).

Investigations and treatment. It is important to find out whether the patient is taking sufficient iron-containing foods, such as meat, green vegetables and eggs in her diet and also whether she is taking her iron and folic acid tablets regularly. If her haemoglobin falls below 115 g/litre (11·5 g per 100 ml), a full investigation will be carried out, including a full blood-picture, serum iron and folate estimations, screening for infection and, very occasionally, a bone-marrow puncture.

The patient may be given iron intramuscularly or intravenously and, in severe cases near term, a blood transfusion may be necessary, though more often blood is cross-matched and given after delivery if required.

Pyelonephritis

Pyelonephritis is an infection involving the upper renal tract and is particularly common in pregnancy, when the ureters and renal pelvis become dilated and urinary stasis occurs. The infection usually occurs after the 20th week and may recur in the puerperium. Routine screening of all pregnant women for asymptomatic bacteriuria and subsequent treatment has markedly reduced the incidence of pyelonephritis in pregnancy, and should reduce chronic renal failure later in life.

Signs and symptoms. The patient complains of loin pain and may also have frequency and pain on micturition. She has a fever, with rigors in severe cases, and complains of a headache, malaise, nausea and vomiting.

Investigations and treatment. The diagnosis is confirmed by finding pus cells and bacteria in a mid-stream specimen of urine. Bed rest, analgesics, copious fluids and antibiotics are prescribed to treat this condition. Continued antibiotic therapy with reduced dosage is sometimes necessary throughout pregnancy to prevent the infection recurring. Follow-up includes haemoglobin estimations and repeated examination of the urine to ensure that it is sterile and, if necessary, further investigation of the renal tract after delivery.

Cardiac disease

There is added strain on the heart in pregnancy because of the increased blood volume, cardiac output and weight gain, but while a normal heart easily meets these demands, a diseased heart may fail.

Heart disease may be classified as:
    Grade I. No symptoms during ordinary activities
    Grade II. Comfortable at rest, but ordinary physical exertion leads to fatigue, palpitations and dyspnoea
    Grade III. Comfortable at rest, but less than ordinary physical exertion leads to dyspnoea and fatigue
    Grade IV. The patient has symptoms of heart failure, even at rest

Most pregnant women with cardiac disease are in grades I and II, but the condition may deteriorate with the additional burden of pregnancy.

Management. The pregnancy is closely supervised by an obstetrician and a cardiologist. Extra rest is essential and is achieved by ensuring that the woman has help in the house and is admitted to hospital about a week before delivery or, if she has symptoms, earlier in her pregnancy. Anaemia must be prevented and any infection treated promptly; the patient is asked to report a cough or any increased dyspnoea which could indicate impending heart failure. Patients in grades III or IV may be advised to undergo cardiac surgery in early pregnancy or perhaps therapeutic abortion.

Labour. It has been noted that most patients with heart disease have quick, easy labours and undue exertion in the second stage is prevented by forceps delivery or vacuum extraction. Antibiotics are usually prescribed in labour and throughout the first week of the puerperium to prevent bacterial endocarditis.

Puerperium. Close observation for signs of cardiac failure and additional rest are necessary. Family planning should be discussed before the patient is discharged from hospital.

Diabetes mellitus

It has been estimated that between 1 and 3 per 1 000 women of child-bearing age are diabetic. The patient may be a known diabetic or the disease may first appear in pregnancy. Any ante-natal patient with glycosuria on two or more occasions should be investigated for diabetes.

Effect of diabetes on pregnancy. Monilial vaginitis is particularly common in diabetic patients, but in the last trimester of pregnancy more serious problems such as pre-eclampsia and polyhydramnios may also develop. The baby tends to be large, often 4-5 kg, the incidence of congenital malformations is increased and the perinatal mortality rate is high, most of the deaths in utero occurring after the 36th week of pregnancy for reasons which are not fully understood

Effect of pregnancy on diabetes. Diabetes tends to become unstable and difficult to control in pregnancy and the patient's insulin requirements increase, especially in the last trimester. Good control of diabetes in essential, however, as it has been shown that the fetal mortality is related to the degree of diabetic control achieved.

Management. The patient should be under the combined care of an obstetrician and physician throughout her pregnancy. It is usually necessary to admit her to hospital early in pregnancy to adjust her diet and insulin requirements, and most patients are again admitted at 32 weeks for the remainder of their pregnancy, as further adjustments and surveillance of blood sugars will be necessary. Labour is induced or the patient delivered by Caesarean section at 36-38 weeks to avoid intrauterine death.

After delivery the mother's insulin requirements fall sharply and care must be taken to prevent hypoglycaemia.

The baby of the diabetic mother

The baby is usually large, though size is related to the degree of control of the diabetes. Despite his size the baby is initially nursed in an incubator in the special care nursery where he can be observed carefully for signs of respiratory distress syndrome and hypoglycaemia. Considerable weight-loss occurs in the first week of life and the baby tends to be lethargic, but after this progress should be normal.

11. The Complications of Labour

In cases of abnormal labour the nursing care is basically the same as described in Chapter 6 and thus only special nursing points will be emphasized in this chapter.

Occipito-posterior position

In about ten per cent. of patients the fetal head is deflexed (erect) at the onset of labour and the fetus is in either the right or the left oocipito-posterior position. Hence, the larger occipito-frontal diameter (11·5 cm) has to negotiate the pelvis and together with the bi-parietal diameter (9·5 cm) does not form a well-fitting presenting part. Occipito-posterior positions are called *malpositions* because, although in the majority of cases labour proceeds normally, in a small proportion labour is prolonged and more difficult.

Diagnosis is made by examination per abdomen when a small depression may be seen at about the level of the umbilicus; the head is high and feels large, and limbs are easily palpable on both sides of the abdomen whereas the back is difficult to feel. The fetal heart sounds may be best heard in the midline or the flank. Diagnosis is confirmed in labour by examination per vaginam when the anterior fontanelle is felt anteriorly in the pelvis.

The effect on labour depends largely on the degree of flexion of the fetal head. If flexion increases, the occiput will reach the pelvic floor first, rotate forwards three-eighths of a circle (135°) and delivery should be normal; if, however, flexion is poor, labour will likely be prolonged because the ill-fitting presenting part results in poor cervical stimulation, inefficient but painful contractions and early rupture of the membranes. The patient often has difficulty in passing urine, a distressing backache and a strong desire to push before the end of the first stage which, if not resisted, may result in cervical oedema and hence further delay.

Management. Active management, or accelerated labour, is now the usual practice when progress is slow (see p. 155). Dehydration and ketosis are avoided by the administration of adequate intravenous fluids. Effective analgesia is essential, epidural anaesthesia being particularly suitable in cases of prolonged labour. The fetal heart and uterine contractions are monitored continuously, where possible, and the maternal condition closely observed. Good nursing care is essential and includes not only attending to the patient's physical needs and comfort, as described in Chapter 6, but also giving her support and encouragement to help to maintain her morale. The patient's husband can also help his wife in practical ways, for instance, by massaging her back during contractions to help to relieve the distressing backache.

Outcome. In most cases the occiput rotates forwards, as already described, and delivery is normal. If the head remains deflexed, however, the sinciput (brow) may reach the pelvic floor first and rotate forward and the baby is then delivered in the persistent occipito posterior position (face to pubes). With good contractions and an episiotomy spontaneous delivery occurs, but if there is delay a forceps delivery or vacuum extraction will be performed.

Deficient flexion may also lead to deep transverse arrest when the head is arrested above the level of the ischial spines with the sagittal suture in the transverse diameter of the pelvis. No further progress will take place until the doctor rotates the head to an anterior position, either manually or with Kiellands forceps, and performs a forceps delivery.

Occasionally, if the head is high and deflexed it may partially extend and become a brow presentation or completely extend to a face presentation.

Malpresentations

The normal presentation is cephalic and occurs in 96 per cent. of cases at term. Malpresentations account for the remaining 4 per cent. and of these 3 per cent. are breeches and 1 per cent. either face, brow or shoulder presentations.

Breech presentation

Breech presentation occurs when the buttocks enter the pelvic brim first. It is common at the beginning of the third trimester, but by the 34th week most fetuses have turned spontaneously to cephalic presentation.

Types of breech presentation.

1. *Breech with extended legs.* This is the commonest type of breech presentation, especially in primigravidae with firm abdominal muscles.
2. *Breech with flexed legs.*
3. *Footling and knee presentations* are uncommon.

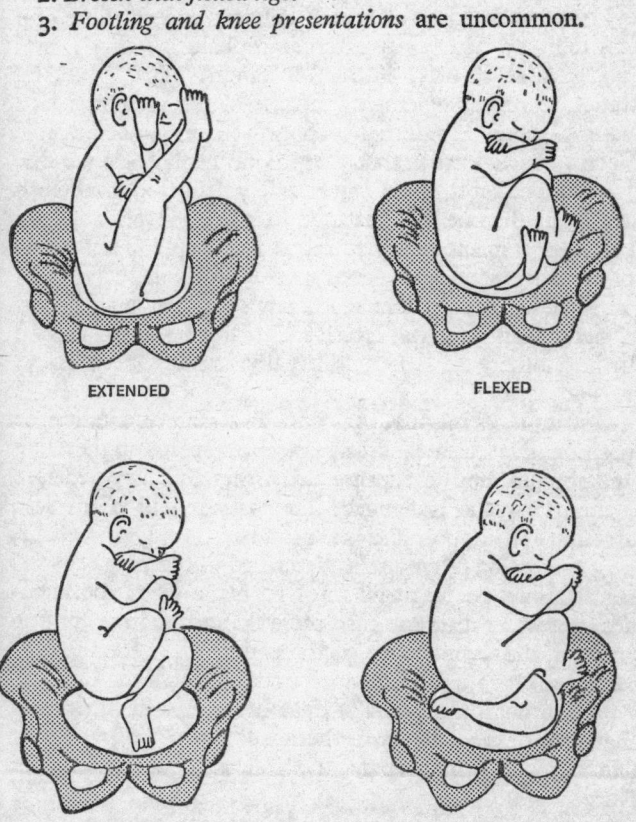

Fig. 24. Types of breech presentation.

Diagnosis. The patient may complain of pain under her ribs in late pregnancy and on palpation the hard, round, ballotable head is found in the fundus of the uterus. If the legs are extended and the breech deeply engaged, however, diagnosis is more difficult as the feet may immobilize the head. The doctor may wish to have the diagnosis confirmed by X-ray or ultrasound.

Management during pregnancy. The obstetrician may attempt to turn the fetus to a cephalic presentation by external cephalic version between the 32nd and 36th weeks of pregnancy, because the risks of breech delivery exceed those of a normal delivery. However, external cephalic version is not without risk as it may, in rare instances, cause placental separation, cord entanglement, rupture of the membranes or premature labour. If external cephalic version is not possible the doctor has to ensure that there is no cephalo-pelvic disproportion and that the baby can be safely delivered as a breech presentation; thus he will make an examination per vaginam for pelvic assessment and may request a lateral X-ray pelvimetry, which shows the antero-posterior diameters of the pelvis. If these investigations reveal any suspicion of a small or abnormally shaped pelvis, elective Caesarean section will be performed, otherwise labour is usually induced between 38 weeks and term.

Management of labour. As with any malpresentation or malposition, there is an ill-fitting presenting part and therefore the membranes tend to rupture early, the cord may prolapse and labour may be prolonged. The patient will need close observation and support and is kept in bed throughout labour, nursing care being otherwise as described in Chapter 6.

Examinations per vaginam must be made when the membranes rupture to diagnose cord prolapse and again to confirm the onset of the second stage, as the patient often has the urge to bear down before full dilatation and, although the buttocks may pass through the partially dilated cervix, difficulties will then arise with the delivery of the head.

The midwife will prepare the following equipment for delivery:
 a forceps delivery trolley, which includes equipment for catheterization, pudendal block, episiotomy and suturing;
 anaesthetic equipment;
 resuscitation equipment for the baby, and a heated incubator; and
 an oxytocic drug.

The patient is placed in the lithotomy position for the delivery, which is conducted by a senior obstetrician. An anaesthetist is present because, if complications arise, the patient may need an immediate anaesthetic, and a paediatrician prepares to resuscitate the baby. When the breech distends the perineum, a catheter is passed to empty the mother's bladder and an episiotomy is performed under pudendal nerve block. The essential principles of delivery are to allow the body to deliver with minimal assistance, but to control the delivery of the head, often with forceps, the whole process taking place without undue delay within about seven minutes.

Dangers of breech delivery. The main dangers are to the baby, and are as follows.

1. *Birth asphyxia*, because the cord is compressed at the pelvic brim when the after-coming head enters the pelvis, thus depriving the baby of oxygen. The resulting hypoxia and handling of the baby may stimulate him to breathe when his head is still in the vagina, and blood and liquor may be inhaled.

2. *Intra-cranial haemorrhage*, due to the rapid compression of the fetal head when it enters the pelvis and sudden release of pressure a few minutes later at delivery.

3. *Injuries* such as fractures, damage to nerves and muscles and, rarely, ruptured abdominal organs.

Face, brow, shoulder presentations

Face presentation

Face presentation occurs when the head is completely extended and the occiput in contact with the fetal back. It may be due to a fetal abnormality such as anencephaly (see Glossary), or occur if the head becomes extended in labour, often following a deflexed occipito-posterior position.

Face presentation may be suspected on examination per abdomen but the diagnosis is usually made upon vaginal examination when the facial landmarks can be felt. If the chin (mentum) is anterior, the patient may deliver spontaneously, whereas if the chin is posterior and fails to rotate forward, labour will become obstructed and a Caesarean section will then be necessary.

At birth the baby's face is bruised and grossly oedematous. His unsightly appearance should be explained to his mother and she should be assured that the bruising and oedema will subside within a few days.

Brow presentation

Brow presentation occurs when the head is partially extended. Vaginal delivery is usually impossible because the large presenting diameter, the mento-vertical measuring 13·5 cm, cannot enter the pelvis; Caesarean section is therefore performed to prevent an obstructed labour.

Shoulder presentation

A shoulder presentation occurs when the lie of the fetus is transverse or oblique. If the lie varies from one examination to another, it is said to be unstable, and the commonest cause is laxity of the uterine and abdominal muscles, as occurs in multiparous patients. Other causes are placenta praevia, pelvic tumour or contracted pelvis, because in all these instances the presenting part is unable to enter the pelvis. It may also occur with polyhydramnios or multiple pregnancy, especially after the birth of the first twin.

Management. The patient is referred to the obstetrician, who will convert the transverse lie to a longitudinal lie by external version, if there is no contra-indication to a vaginal delivery. This may have to be repeated several times, as the lie may revert to transverse or oblique. At 38 weeks the patient is usually admitted to hospital to await the onset of labour, because early rupture of the membranes is likely and the cord or an arm could prolapse and labour become obstructed. If the lie cannot be corrected at the onset or in labour, an immediate Caesarean section is essential to avoid an obstructed labour.

Cephalo-pelvic disproportion

Cephalo-pelvic disproportion is present when the head is too large or the pelvis too small for the head to engage. It is most common in primigravidae, but may also occur in multigravid patients as the fetus tends to increase in size in successive pregnancies. Primigravidae in whom the fetal head is not engaged by the 36th–38th weeks of pregnancy should be referred to an obstetrician; likewise a multigravida with a particularly large baby, poor obstetric history or head which cannot be made to engage.

Investigations carried out by the obstetrician include examination per abdomen to decide on the degree of disproportion, examination per vaginam for pelvic assessment, and probably a lateral X-ray pelvimetry which shows the anterio-posterior diameters of the pelvis.

Management. If cephalo-pelvic disproportion is diagnosed, the patient will have to be delivered by Caesarean section, unless it is of a minor degree when the patient may have a trial labour. Trial labour is an ordinary labour, conducted in hospital under the care of an obstetrician, to see if the head will become engaged. If the head engages, labour then proceeds normally, whereas if the head fails to engage despite good uterine contractions, Caesarean section is performed.

Obstructed labour

Obstructed labour occurs when the fetus cannot pass through the pelvis in spite of good uterine contractions. Possible causes are a contracted pelvis, pelvic tumour, malpresentations such as shoulder or brow, deep transverse arrest or a particularly large or abnormal baby.

Diagnosis. There is no progress in labour despite strong, painful contractions which cause excessive retraction and thickening of the upper segment and abnormal thinning of the lower segment; thus the physiological retraction ring becomes markedly accentuated and is visible abdominally. Eventually the contractions may become almost continuous, the fetus dies from anoxia and, unless urgent action is taken, the uterus will rupture and the mother will also die.

Management. Obstructed labour should be avoided with good ante-natal care and management of labour. If it does occur, however, morphine 15 mg or a general anaesthetic is given to reduce the force of uterine contractions and the patient delivered as soon as possible, usually by Caesarean section.

Induction of labour

Induction of labour is usually carried out, when required, between the 38th and 42nd week of pregnancy, though earlier induction may be necessary if the health or life of the mother or fetus are endangered if pregnancy continues. Failure is more likely with early inductions, especially before the 36th week, and therefore Caesarean section may be preferable.

Indications for induction:

post-maturity, 41 weeks or more
pre-eclampsia and eclampsia (see pp. 132–136)
ante-partum haemorrhage (see pp. 136–140)
placental insufficiency (see p. 141)
poor obstetric history
minor degree of cephalo-pelvic disproportion
medical conditions such as:
    chronic hypertension
    renal disease
    diabetes
intra-uterine death
fetal abnormality
breech presentation (see pp. 148–151)
rhesus incompatibility (see p. 125)
large baby

Methods of induction

Oxytocic drugs

(a) **Syntocinon** is given intravenously to induce labour, either via an automatic infusion unit or a manually controlled infusion, often started with two units of Syntocinon in 500 ml of 5 per cent. dextrose solution (25 g) at 10 drops per minute and gradually increased to a maximum of 60 drops per minute. When labour is established, the infusion rate is no longer increased.

(b) **Buccal pitocin,** administered at half-hourly intervals, the tablets being placed between the gum and cheek where they are gradually absorbed. Intravenous oxytocin, however, is safer as it is more quickly and easily controlled.

(c) **Prostaglandin E2** may be administered orally or intravenously in gradually increasing doses to induce labour. However, side effects such as vomiting and diarrhoea may occur and, when administered intravenously, local tissue reaction.

When oxytocic drugs are used the patient must be under constant supervision as powerful, prolonged contractions may occur which could cause fetal hypoxia or even rupture of the uterus. Continuous monitoring of the fetal heart and contractions is desirable, otherwise quarter-hourly observations are essential and should also include pulse, blood pressure and vaginal loss.

Surgical induction

This artificial rupture of the membranes is the most certain method of inducing labour, especially when used in conjunction with oxytocic drugs, as is usually the case. If the presenting part is high, however, the membranes should not be ruptured, because of the risk of the cord prolapsing. The procedure is explained to the patient, who may be given a premedication if she is very apprehensive. She is prepared for labour, empties her bladder and is placed in the lithotomy position. The fetal heart sounds are listened to, and under strict aseptic conditions the doctor then passes two fingers through the cervix and ruptures the membranes with Kocher's forceps. The colour of the liquor is noted and the fetal heart is auscultated immediately after induction and thereafter continuous or frequent recordings are made. Sterile vulval pads are applied as the risk of infection is now increased. Labour usually starts soon after the membranes are ruptured and the oxytocic infusion is commenced, but on the rare occasions when induction fails, Caesarean section becomes necessary.

Active management of labour

Active management, or accelerated labour, is now the usual practice when progress is slow, and involves examination per vaginam to diagnose the onset of labour and subsequently at regular intervals to assess progress, with cervical dilatation being plotted on a partograph. Slow progress can then be detected early and labour accelerated by artificial rupture of membranes and, perhaps, by oxytocic drugs, usually intravenous Syntocinon. Very careful monitoring of both maternal and fetal condition is then essential. With this active management, few patients are in labour longer than 12 hours and most will have a normal delivery. If active management fails to accelerate the progress of labour, or fetal hypoxia develops, an operative delivery will be necessary.

Cord presentation and prolapse

Presentation of the cord occurs when the cord lies below the presenting part in intact membranes; when the membranes rupture the cord is then described as **prolapsed**. There is a high fetal mortality when the cord prolapses partly because it becomes compressed between the presenting part and the cervix or pelvic wall, thus cutting off the oxygen supply to the fetus, and partly because any interference, e g even cold if it slips out of the vulva, or handling, is enough to stop the flow of oxygenated blood returning to the fetus.

Causes. Cord presentation and prolapse are most likely to occur when there is an ill-fitting presenting part and a long cord. The presenting part does not fit snugly into the lower uterine segment if the head is high due to multiparity, polyhydramnios or cephalo-pelvic disproportion, and when malpresentations or malpositions occur, or the baby is small.

Diagnosis. The cord may be visible at the vulva or felt on examination per vaginam.

Management. If the fetus is alive immediate delivery is essential, by Caesarean section in the first stage of labour or forceps delivery in the second stage. Whilst urgent preparations for delivery are being made, the foot of the bed is elevated or the patient placed in the knee-chest position to relieve pressure on the cord. Pressure may be further relieved by the midwife pushing the presenting part up with two fingers placed in the vagina. The mother may be given oxygen to inhale until her baby is safely delivered and the cord, if visible, must be kept warm.

Fetal distress

Lack of oxygen (hypoxia) to the fetus in utero may produce the following signs of fetal distress:

   (a) a marked change in fetal heart rate of approximately 20 beats per minute or more;

   (b) irregularity of the fetal heart beat;

(c) late deceleration, when the fetal heart slows at the end or immediately after contractions: this is most easily diagnosed when continuous fetal heart monitoring is carried out and is a serious sign of fetal distress;

(d) meconium-stained liquor;

(e) convulsive fetal movements, which occur with severe hypoxia.

Causes: The main causes can be considered under the following headings.

Cord. If the cord prolapses, becomes entangled around the fetus or tightly knotted, the oxygen supply to the fetus will be reduced.

Placenta. Conditions such as placental insufficiency, postmaturity or premature separation all interfere with the supply of oxygen to the fetus.

Uterus. Hypertonic uterine contractions are abnormally long and strong, and the uterus has a high resting-tone between contractions, which interferes with placental circulation and therefore the supply of oxygen to the fetus.

Maternal conditions such as anaemia, severe cardiac disease or hypertension may result in a diminished oxygen supply to the fetus.

Fetal conditions which may lead to hypoxia include severe haemolytic disease, intra-cranial injury and some congenital malformations.

Management. The doctor is informed and the fetal heart monitored continuously or with each contraction. The mother is turned onto her side to improve the placental circulation and may be given oxygen. An examination per vaginam is carried out to diagnose the exact stage of labour and exclude possible cord prolapse. In the first stage the doctor may obtain a fetal blood sample for pH estimation by making a small incision in the fetal scalp. Hypoxia causes acidosis (blood is more acid) and the pH therefore falls; if the pH falls below 7·25 (normal 7·35), the baby is delivered immediately by Caesarean section to avoid intra-uterine death. Fetal distress most commonly occurs in the second stage, however, when a forceps delivery can be performed or, if delivery is imminent, an episiotomy may suffice.

Resuscitation equipment should be prepared and a paediatician be present to receive the baby at birth.

Delay in the second stage

Steady progress should normally be made during the second stage of labour with delivery within one hour for primigravidae and half an hour for multigravidae. However, delivery may be delayed for the following reasons:

Fetal factors: a large baby
malposition or malpresentation (see pp. 147-152)
fetal abnormality
Maternal factors: full bladder or rectum
rigid perineum
fatigue
weak uterine contractions (hypotonic)
contracted pelvis

Management. The doctor is informed; he will review the patient's history, assess her general condition, pelvic size and progress in labour and then perform either a forceps delivery, vacuum extraction, or, possibly, Caesarean section.

Post-partum haemorrhage

Primary post-partum haemorrhage is defined as excessive bleeding from the genital tract occurring in the first 24 hours after the delivery of the baby, the amount of blood loss usually being 500 ml or more. Excessive bleeding occurring more than 24 hours and up to about six weeks after delivery is termed secondary post-partum haemorrhage (see p. 164).

Causes. The main cause of post-partum haemorrhage (P P H) is a uterus which fails to contract and retract efficiently (i e atonic), thus the uterine blood vessels are inadequately compressed by the muscle fibres and bleeding occurs from the placental site. This is most likely to occur with:

a multiparous patient with lax uterine muscles
multiple pregnancy: not only are the uterine muscles over-stretched but there is also a larger placental site
polyhydramnios, because the uterine muscles are over-distended
prolonged labour
retained placenta or residual products of conception ⎫
fibroids ⎬ interference with efficient uterine action
full bladder ⎭

ante-partum haemorrhage (see p. 140)
general anaesthesia – may diminish uterine action
anaemia
mismanagement of the third stage.

Prevention. Every effort is made to prevent post-partum haemorrhage by good ante-natal care to ensure that the patient's general health is good and that she is not anaemic. Prolonged labour, dehydration and a full bladder should be avoided and an oxytocic drug administered at the time of delivery to reduce the risk of haemorrhage. Any patient who is particularly likely to bleed excessively should be delivered in hospital under the care of a consultant obstetrician and will be given intravenous ergometrine 0·5 mg during the delivery.

Management. The uterus is massaged to stimulate a contraction and an oxytocic drug administered. If still in situ, the placenta is then delivered by controlled cord traction; if bleeding persists a catheter is passed to empty the bladder and bi-manual compression may be carried out, that is, the uterus is compressed between the two hands placed on the abdomen. An intravenous infusion would be set up by the doctor to which Syntocinon 10–20 units could be added to stimulate uterine contractions, and blood is cross-matched ready for transfusion. If the placenta cannot be delivered, it is removed manually under a general anaesthetic by the doctor.

Traumatic post-partum haemorrhage

This bleeding from lacerations of the genital tract should be suspected if bleeding occurs when the uterus is well contracted. The treatment is to suture the lacerations.

Any woman who has had a post-partum haemorrhage needs close observation and reassurance; she should be booked into a consultant unit for her confinement in any future pregnancy.

Prolonged third stage

The placenta and membranes are usually delivered within a few minutes of the birth of the baby, but occasionally there is a delay, when the third stage is then said to be prolonged.

Causes. The commonest causes are hypotonic (weak) uterine action, a full bladder and faulty technique in the management of the third stage. A constriction ring may occur, when a band of circular muscle fibres in the uterus goes into spasm, and the placenta is retained above or within this tight band. Very rarely, the placenta is embedded in the uterine muscle (placenta accreta); the treatment for this is hysterectomy.

Management. The dangers of a prolonged third stage are haemorrhage and shock; thus the doctor should be informed if the placenta is not delivered within 20 minutes, or earlier if bleeding occurs. If after catheterization to empty the bladder the placenta is still undelivered, preparations must be made for a manual removal of placenta and membranes under general anaesthetic. Because of the risk of haemorrhage, an intravenous infusion is set up and blood cross-matched before carrying out this procedure.

Operative deliveries

Most women deliver their babies by their own expulsive efforts in the second stage of labour, but sometimes problems arise which necessitate operative delivery.

Forceps delivery

Indications. Maternal indications are hypertension, cardiac disease and a prolonged second stage. Fetal indications include signs of hypoxia, the after-coming head of a breech, and deep transverse arrest or a persistent occipito-posterior position (see p. 148).

Procedure. After explaining the procedure to the patient, she is placed in the lithotomy position and the doctor makes an examination per vaginam, using aseptic technique, to ensure that conditions are suitable for a forceps delivery. The cervix must be fully dilated, the outlet of the pelvis adequate and the position of the head identified. Adequate analgesia is usually achieved by a pudendal nerve block (see p. 162) and perineal infiltration for episiotomy, inhalational analgesia being administered by a midwife who remains beside the patient. A catheter is passed to empty the bladder and the obstetric forceps are then applied, one on each side of the fetal head, thus forming a protective cage for it. The doctor can then apply traction to deliver the baby safely, having performed an episiotomy when the head distends the perineum to prevent damage to the mother's soft tissues.

Vacuum extraction (Ventouse)

The Ventouse extractor consists of a suction cup connected to a vacuum pump by a rubber tube, through which a chain passes. The cup is attached to the fetal scalp by creating a vacuum which draws the scalp into the cavity of the cup. When the cup is firmly fixed, the doctor exerts traction on the chain with each contraction, thus hastening the delivery of the baby. The baby will have a large chignon, or pad of oedema, on his head at birth, which subsides within two or three days. Occasionally the vacuum extractor is applied towards the end of the first stage to hasten full dilatation of the cervix.

The indications and preparations of the patient for vacuum extraction are as for forceps delivery.

Caesarean section

The baby is delivered by abdominal operation, the uterine incision being made in the lower segment, mainly because there involution does not interfere with healing. The name stems from a Roman law, the Lex Caesarea, which directed that the child should be removed from any woman who died in childbirth.

Indications. There are many indications for Caesarean section, the main ones being:

disproportion (pp. 152-153)
ante-partum haemorrhage (pp. 138-140)
severe pre-eclampsia and eclampsia (pp. 134-135)
malpresentations, breech, brow, shoulder (pp. 150-152)
prolonged labour (pp. 155-156)
fetal distress (pp. 156-157)
diabetes, in some cases (p. 146)
two or more previous Caesarean sections

Preparation. Caesarean section may be elective (planned) but is commonly an emergency operation. Preparation includes an abdominal and pubic shave and, except in emergency cases, suppositories or an enema followed by a bath or shower. A catheter must be inserted and left in situ, as the bladder must be emptied immediately prior to the operation. Premedication is given, as ordered by the anaesthetist.

Post-operative care is as for any patient following a major abdominal operation, but in addition the lochia are observed and particular attention must be paid to vulval hygiene. Postnatal breast care is carried out, remembering that lactation usually takes longer to become established post-operatively. The mother should see and have as much contact with her baby as possible during the early post-operative period, though it may be several days before she is well enough to start caring for him.

Obstetric anaesthesia

General anaesthesia is particularly dangerous in obstetric patients because of the risk of Mendelson's syndrome. This condition occurs when the patient inhales vomit under anaesthesia, because highly-acid gastric fluid may enter the lungs and cause intense bronchiolar spasm and an outpouring of fluid into the alveoli. Mendelson's syndrome may be fatal, and measures to prevent it are essential; they include dietary restriction and antacid therapy in labour. As the stomach empties very slowly during labour, solid food is withheld and fluids only are given once labour is established. In cases of abnormal labour, when the administration of a general anaesthetic is more likely, intravenous fluids only are given. All patients are given an alkali such as magnesium trisilicate 15 ml two hourly throughout labour and immediately before a general anaesthetic to reduce the acidity of the stomach.

Pudendal nerve block

Because of the hazards of general anaesthesia in obstetric patients, regional anaesthesia is considered preferable for many operative procedures. Pudendal nerve block abolishes pain sensation in the vulva, vagina and much of the perineum and is suitable in most cases for forceps deliveries, vacuum extractions, breech deliveries and the repair of episiotomies. A local anaesthetic, usually 10 ml of 1 per cent. lignocaine (100 mg), is injected around each pudendal nerve just behind the ischial spines a few minutes before the operative procedure is carried out. In addition, infiltration of the perineum with local anaesthetic solution is also required. (For epidural anaesthesia see p. 78).

12. The Complications of the Puerperium

Most women suffer from some discomfort during the early days of the puerperium, but occasionally more serious disorders occur.

Complications of the genital tract

Infection. The large open wound of the placental site, and any bruised, lacerated tissues of the genital tract, predispose to infection as they provide the ideal conditions in which microorganisms thrive. The causative organisms are mainly Escherichia coli, staphylococci, anaerobic streptococci and Clostridium welchii.

The patient who develops a local uterine infection, usually on the third or fourth day post-partum, will have a raised temperature and pulse rate, offensive lochia and general malaise. The uterus is often large and soft (sometimes called subinvoluted), and may be tender on palpation. Immediate treatment is necessary to prevent the now rare event of the infection spreading from the primary site to cause salpingitis, pelvic cellulitis, peritonitis or septicaemia. Thrombophlebitis of the uterine veins may occur and the infected clots, known as emboli, may travel in the blood stream and lodge in the lungs and other organs.

Management. After a review of her history, the patient is examined by the doctor and a cervical swab, mid-stream specimen of urine, and nose and throat swabs are taken and sent to the laboratory for culture and sensitivities. In more serious cases a blood culture, blood count and chest X-ray may also be required.

The patient is isolated and the infection treated with a broad-spectrum antibiotic. Vulval hygiene is particularly important and observations should include temperature, pulse rate, lochia and the condition of the uterus. Depression, usually mild, is a common feature of puerperal infections; thus the mother will require much care and understanding. She should have as much contact with her baby as possible, though the midwife will care for him until she is well enough.

Secondary post-partum haemorrhage (see p. 158). Secondary post-partum haemorrhage is caused mainly by retained placental tissue or infection. The management is to massage the uterus, if palpable, to cause it to contract, to give ergometrine 0·5 mg or syntometrine 1 ml intra-muscularly, to encourage the patient to empty her bladder and to send for the doctor. A digital exploration of the uterus under general anaesthesia may be necessary to remove retained placental tissue, although if infection is suspected, this may be deferred until sufficient antibiotics have been given.

Complications of the urinary tract

Infection is particularly likely in patients who have had pyelonephritis during pregnancy or who were catheterized in labour (see p. 144).

Retention of urine also predisposes to infection and may be caused if bruising or prolonged overstretching of the urethra and overdistension of the bladder have occurred in labour. Laxity of the abdominal muscles and a sore perineum after delivery may also cause difficulty with micturition. If the bladder becomes too full, the patient may have retention with overflow.

Treatment is continuous bladder drainage for two or three days to allow the tone of the bladder to be restored and any bruising and oedema of the urethra and bladder neck to subside. The patient should be encouraged to drink copious fluids and may be given potassium citrate mixture 15 ml four-hourly to reduce the risk of infection.

Incontinence of urine may occur in multiparous women due to a lax pelvic floor. The immediate treatment is pelvic floor exercises which improve the muscle tone and may rectify the condition, though in some instances operative measures may be required months or years later.

Very rarely, the cause of incontinence may be a vesicovaginal fistula which develops between the bladder and vagina if the bladder is damaged in labour; this requires expert surgical attention.

Breast disorders

Mastitis is a breast infection occurring during or after the second week of the puerperium and is usually caused by the staphylococcus aureus. The organisms enter the breast through a crack in the nipple or through the ducts if the baby is harbouring staphylococci in his nose. A painful, red, wedge-shaped area of inflammation develops in the breast which, if not treated, may lead to the formation of an abscess. The axillary glands become enlarged, the patient is pyrexial and complains of a general malaise which feels rather like the onset of influenza.

Prevention. If the nipples become sore or cracked, breast feeding is stopped for 24–48 hours on the affected side to allow the nipple to heal. A lanolin-based cream is applied to the nipples or, in the case of a cracked nipple, one application of tincture of benzoin to aid healing.

Treatment of mastitis is to take specimens of milk from both breasts and send to the laboratory for culture and sensitivity testing, and the doctor will prescribe an antibiotic. The milk from both breasts is then expressed four hourly and discarded, the baby being given supplementary feeds. Sometimes a single dose of ethinyl oestradiol 0·1–0·2 mg is given to reduce temporarily the production of milk. The patient is nursed in bed, given a light, nourishing diet and analgesics, as prescribed. If the infection begins to respond to treatment after 24 hours, the baby can be fed on the non-infected breast and, when no sign of infection remains, is then fully breast fed again.

Excess milk causing over-filling of the breasts. Over-filling of the breasts may occur between the third and the fifth day, but this problem can often be avoided by careful antenatal assessment and the use of prophylactic ethinyl oestradiol started within 24 hours of delivery (see p. 110). Palliative measures include hot bathing before feeds, the use of a Syntocinon spray to improve milk flow, help with fixing the baby to the breast and expression of surplus milk after feeds. A diuretic such as frusemide (Lasix) 40 mg and ethinyl oestradiol 0·1–0·2 mg are sometimes prescribed. Analgesics and a firm, supporting binder will help to ease the discomfort.

Insufficient milk. It is normally at least three or four days before the breasts produce sufficient milk for the baby. If lactation subsequently becomes inadequate, it is important to ensure that the mother has enough rest, a good diet, adequate fluids and is free from worry. The baby is given complementary feeds, and, if the mother can relax, content in knowing that her baby is having adequate feeds, her milk supply may gradually improve.

Engorgement. Engorgement occurs when the veins and lymphatic vessels are overfilled, the stasis leading to marked oedema and inhibition of milk flow. It occurs between the third and fifth day, is extremely painful and needs sympathetic and skilful handling. The patient is given an immediate dose of ethinyl oestradiol 0·4 mg, and usually frusemide (Lasix) 40–80 mg. The breasts are gently hot-bathed, or ice packs may be comforting, but no attempt should be made to express milk or put the baby to the breast until the milk flow recommences spontaneously. A firm binder is applied and analgesics are given as required.

Thrombo-embolic disorders

Thrombophlebitis occurs when a clot has formed in an inflamed and often varicose, superficial vein. The clot is firmly attached to the vein, however, and is usually reabsorbed, therefore pulmonary embolism rarely occurs. The patient has a slight rise in temperature and pulse rate and complains of pain in her leg, the inflamed vein being visible. Treatment is ambulation and the wearing of support tights.

Phlebothrombosis is a very serious condition which occurs when there is clot formation in the deep veins of the pelvis or legs and a risk of fragments becoming detached and causing a pulmonary embolism. The patient has a raised temperature and pulse rate, complains of pain in her leg or groin, and the leg is swollen and tense.

Treatment. Anticoagulant therapy is commenced to prevent further clotting, but the lochia must be carefully observed because of the likelihood of bleeding from the placental site. The patient is usually nursed in bed until the pain has subsided, with the foot of the bed elevated and a cradle provided to take the weight of the bedclothes off the legs. Analgesics are given, and antibiotics are prescribed if pelvic infection is suspected. The legs are well supported when ambulation becomes possible.

Pulmonary embolism is one of the major causes of maternal death in the United Kingdom. In only a few cases is there any clinical evidence of venous thrombosis, the majority occurring without any warning. Early ambulation or, where this is not possible, movement in bed is an essential preventive measure for all patients following delivery. Immediate resuscitative treatment includes the administration of oxygen and an anticoagulant drug intravenously.

Puerpural psychosis

Puerpural psychosis is an abnormal mental state following childbirth, commonest in patients with a history of mental instability. Women who have had a traumatic pregnancy or labour or who develop puerperal sepsis seem especially prone to mental illness.

Persistent insomnia is an important early sign. The patient may be talkative or withdrawn and show signs of irrational or obsessional behaviour. Abject depression or violent behaviour with manic outbursts may occur and the patient could injure herself or her baby.

Early recognition and referral to a psychiatrist is necessary. Treatment may be prolonged, but the prognosis is usually good.

13. Family Planning

Family planning is an important part of the care of mothers and children for two main reasons:
1. to ensure every child is given the best possible start in life by being planned for and wanted;
2. in order that maternal health and family happiness are not threatened by the birth of too many children or children born too closely together.

Nearly all couples will need family planning advice at some time, and it is important for nurses to recognize this need in a wide variety of situations, but nurses who are involved in the care of mothers during pregnancy, childbirth, and the postnatal period have a special opportunity and a special responsibility to help.

A wide variety of contraceptive methods is available and family planning services are now an integral part of the National Health Service; advice and supplies are available free of charge from family planning clinics and family doctors. Many people are, however, still ignorant of what is available and too shy to ask for help; those most in need of contraceptive advice are often the least likely to be able to obtain it. It is important therefore for the nurse to take the initiative in raising the subject. During pregnancy and the puerperium there will be many opportunities for her to do so but the post-natal examination should always include specific discussion about contraception. In some post-natal clinics a method can be prescribed or a device fitted on the spot; if this is not possible, referral to a family planning clinic or to the woman's own general practitioner can be arranged. A woman can become pregnant again within a few weeks of giving birth. Ovulation may recommence as early as three weeks after delivery, and since it will occur *before* menstruation, a woman can become pregnant again even before her first period after childbirth. Contraception is therefore required as soon as intercourse begins again, and a temporary method may be needed even before the post-natal examination. In many maternity hospitals nowadays a family planning doctor or nurse will visit the wards to offer information and advice to new mothers.

Family size and family spacing

Couples have varying attitudes concerning the number of children they want and it is their right to have as few or as many as they wish; the important factor is that each child should be wanted. However, we do know that too many pregnancies may damage a mother's health, and the incidence of complications such as hypertension and haemorrhage rises with increasing age and parity. The child of the large family is also at risk, even before birth. The perinatal mortality rate increases with the mother's age and parity; a study in Newcastle in 1963 found that the rate increased from 24 per 1 000 for first babies to 34 for fourth babies, 50 for fifth babies and 90 for eighth babies. The disadvantages continue long after birth; several studies have demonstrated that children of large families are smaller and lighter, are less well nourished, have a lower reading age and do less well at school than children of smaller families, and that these disadvantages are independent of social class.

The interval between pregnancies is also important. If pregnancies follow in too rapid a succession the mother's body has no chance to recover between them. In particular, she may not replace the stores of iron which become depleted with repeated pregnancies and so she becomes anaemic. Anaemia increases the risks of complications during a subsequent confinement and causes chronic fatigue and ill-health. The risks are greatest when the interval between the end of one pregnancy and the beginning of the next is less than a year, i e when the age gap between children is less than about 21 months.

Several births in quick succession means several babies all competing at the same times for the same kind of maternal attention, and from a mother who is debilitated by the physical and emotional demands of pregnancy and the sheer physical and mental fatigue caused by constant broken nights and coping with the practicalities of baby care. In such a situation the whole family suffers.

Table 5. Methods of Contraception

Method	How It Works	How It Is Used
Hormonal Methods Combined pill (oestrogen and progesterone)	Inhibits ovulation by acting on pituitary gland to suppress gonadotrophins	taken orally, fixed regime based on 28-day cycle; each course followed by withdrawal bleeding
Progesterone-only pill	(i) alteration in cervical mucus to prevent sperm entry (ii) impaired endometrial development	taken orally; taken continuously at the same time every day; no break as with combined pill
Injectable progesterone	as progesterone-only pill; slow release	deep intramuscular injection at intervals of 3, 6, or 12 months
Barrier Methods Occlusive cap	rubber cap covers cervix creating mechanical barrier between ovum and spermatozoa	inserted into vagina before intercourse, removed not less than 6 hours afterwards; must be used with spermicidal cream
Sheath (condom, french letter, protective etc)	fits closely over erect penis trapping sperms inside	rolled over erect penis before intercourse; must be put on before any genital contact; penis must be carefully withdrawn while still erect to avoid leakage; use once only unless of special washable kind
Spermicidal chemicals (cream, pessaries, foaming tablets, aerosol foam, C-film)	kills spermatozoa	inserted into vagina using finger or special applicator

Disadvantages	Advantages	Points To Note
Small risk of thrombosis (risk of death less than $\frac{1}{20}$ of that from causes associated with pregnancy); unsuitable for a few women on medical grounds; occasional side effects, e g headache	most reliable method available; beneficial side effects include regular light, painless periods; timing not related to sexual activity	motivation important: the woman must remember to take it; side effects widely publicised and unduly emphasized, greatly reduced by introduction of new, low-dose pills
Irregular menstrual bleeding; less reliable than the combined pill	avoids side effects of combined pill which are mainly due to oestrogenic component; useful for breast-feeding mothers in whom 'combined' pill may reduce lactation	must be taken at same time every day, including during menstruation; protection is reduced if interval between tablets varies
as for progesterone-only pill; speed of release uncertain	useful where motivation to persist with other methods is poor; useful following husband's vasectomy until semen tests are negative	not yet widely available
must be inserted before each intercourse; must be fitted initially by doctor or nurse; unsuitable for some women for anatomical, emotional (e g inhibition about 'touching themselves'), or aesthetic reasons ('messy'); unsuitable for immediate post-natal period	no harmful side effects; does not reduce sexual sensation—undetectable in use if correctly fitted and inserted; easy to use once learnt; under direct control of the woman—preferred by some for this reason	diaphragm most commonly used, but several kinds available; motivation important—failure is often due to failure to use cap correctly or on every occasion; good teaching essential to establish patient's confidence
cannot be put on before erection, therefore interrupts love-play; may reduce sexual sensation; occasionally produces local allergic reaction	widely available without medical involvement; no harmful side-effects; suitable where man wants to take contraceptive responsibility; very useful as temporary method during immediate post-natal period, while awaiting I U D insertion, etc	great variety of brands available, quality controlled by British Standard (kite-mark); reliability improved if used with chemical spermicide; may give some protection against venereal disease
rendered less effective by dilution in the vagina; very unreliable if used alone	widely available without medical involvement	follow manufacturers' instructions carefully; not recommended for use alone, increases reliability of other methods when used with them; essential with occlusive cap

Table 5. (cont.) Methods of Contraception

Method	How It Works	How It Is Used
IUD (intra-uterine device)	exact mechanism unknown; alters endometrium to make it hostile to implantation	inserted by doctor through the cervix into the uterine cavity
Rhythm Method Calendar method	intercourse avoided when ovum is present	time of ovulation estimated from records of previous menstrual cycles; margin of several days before and after ovulation included in 'unsafe' period
Temperature method	intercourse avoided when ovum is present	time of ovulation estimated from slight rise in temp. which occurs immediately after ovulation; woman records her basal temp. daily and couple refrain from intercourse until the temp. rise has been maintained for three days
Sterilization Vasectomy	division of the vas deferens prevents sperm reaching the urethra; the ejaculate therefore contains no sperm to fertilize the ovum	through incision in each side of the scrotum the vas is divided, a small piece is removed, and the ends are ligated; operation usually performed under local anaesthesia
Tubal ligation or laparoscopic sterilization	division of the Fallopian tubes prevents the ovum from reaching the uterus	through an abdominal incision the Fallopian tubes are divided and the ends ligated, or (in laparoscopic sterilization) divided by cautery; both kinds of operation are normally performed under general anaesthesia

Disadvantages	Advantages	Points To Note
may cause heavy or prolonged menstruation; most devices are unsuitable for nulliparous women; a few women are unable to retain the device	effective from time of insertion even without follow-up care, therefore suitable for the poorly-motivated; unrelated to sexual activity, therefore permits spontaneity of love-making	several devices available, some contain copper which enhances effectiveness; may be inserted immediately after delivery or abortion, but expulsion then more common
very unreliable because ovulation is unpredictable; temperature method more reliable because more precise estimate possible; limits intercourse to relatively few days in the month; unsuitable for post-natal period and during menopause	the only method approved by the Roman Catholic Church; some couples feel that the discipline involved strengthens the marital relationship	needs very careful teaching and explanation, and very high motivation; some non-catholic couples use this in conjunction with other methods, e g use contraceptive measures only during the estimated fertile time, or increase their precautions, e g using chemical with IUD
must be considered irreversible, although reanastomosis is occasionally successful	completely reliable; spontaneous anastomosis is very rare	sterility not immediate—stored semen must be used first, therefore contraception still needed until semen tests show no sperm; no effect on sexual performance or sensation —amount and appearance of ejaculate remain the same
must be considered irreversible, although reanastomosis is occasionally successful; requires general anaesthesia; requires admission to hospital, although laparoscopy reduces stay to 24 hours or less		careful counselling of both partners needed before decision to sterilize is reached

Methods of contraception

Only a brief account can be given here; more detailed information may be obtained by consulting one of the books mentioned in the Suggestions for Further Reading.

The methods summarized in Table 5 are the most commonly used reliable methods of contraception, but there are others, and there is some truth in the argument that any method is better than none. Probably the most commonly used method of all is coitus interruptus or 'withdrawal' (often described by patients as 'being careful'). The man simply withdraws his penis from the woman's vagina just before ejaculation so that no sperms are deposited in the vagina. The method is, however, very unreliable because ejaculation is very difficult to control, and some sperm may be released before the penis is withdrawn or may be present at the tip of the urethra even before intercourse begins.

Douching is still used by some women for personal hygiene and as an attempt at contraception. It should always be discouraged; it is useless as a contraceptive measure and may damage the vaginal mucosa.

Breast feeding may delay the return of ovulation after the birth of a baby, but the length of time before ovulation begins again varies greatly from woman to woman. Although it is true that a breast feeding mother may be less likely to conceive than a mother who is bottle-feeding, a reliable method of contraception is still needed.

There are many old wives' tales about contraception which the nurse needs to correct. Many men and women who have a good idea of the physiology of birth do not understand the physiology of conception.

Choosing a method of contraception

The ideal contraceptive would be:
1. 100 per cent. reliable
2. entirely free from side effects
3. pleasant, easy and convenient for both partners to use
4. easily available
5. very cheap – preferably free

Unfortunately, although contraceptives of various kinds have been used for thousands of years, the ideal contraceptive has yet to be invented. However, a great variety of methods is available, and each individual couple must be helped to find the method which suits them best. In making a choice two factors have to be balanced one against the other:
1. acceptability
2. effectiveness.

Acceptability

People's feelings about contraception are as complex as, and are closely related to, their feelings about sex. Such attitudes are affected by factors such as their cultural background, race, religion, age, whether or not they are married, how long they have been married, family size and spacing, their feelings about the male and female roles in marriage and in their sexual relationships, and many other factors. Sometimes these factors operate at an unconscious level so that a woman may not be able to explain even to herself why she 'doesn't like' a particular method. The situation is always doubly complicated because a sexual relationship involves two people, and one partner's feelings about contraception may differ from the other's.

Table 6. Reported Failure Rates for Contraceptive Methods

Method	Pregnancies per 100 WomanYears (Pearl Index)	
	Highest estimate	Lowest estimate
Foam tablets	43	12
Coitus interruptus	38	10
Rhythm method	38	0
Diaphragm	35	4
Sheath	28	7
IUD	3·3	2
Oral contraceptive	1·3	0

Effectiveness

The effectiveness of a contraceptive method depends not only on the method itself but also on the way it is used. For example, a diaphragm (see Table 5) is an effective method only if it is correctly inserted and used in conjunction with a spermicidal cream. A pregnancy occurring in spite of contraception may be due to failure either of method or user.

The effectiveness of various contraceptive methods is shown in Table 6. The wide range for some methods reflects the importance of user failure; for example the success of the rhythm method depends a great deal on the strength of the motivation of the couple using it.

The compromise between effectiveness and acceptability

The most effective method of contraception is not necessarily the best for a particular couple; both medical and personal factors influence the choice. For example, oral contraceptives are undesirable for a few women on purely medical grounds; poor muscle tone after repeated deliveries might make a diaphragm difficult to keep in place; a few women are allergic to rubber or to certain kinds of spermicide. For a woman who cannot be relied on to remember to take a pill every night, an intra-uterine device (I U D) might in the end have a lower failure rate. To some couples it is important that the man should take the responsibility for contraception, for others that it should be the woman. Some Roman Catholics who would reject barrier methods or an I U D can accept the pill because it interferes with ovulation rather than fertilization, while others can accept only the rhythm method. In some cultures a woman who is menstruating is considered 'unclean' and so an intra-uterine device which may cause longer or heavier periods would be unsuitable. Many couples do not want to involve a doctor at all and prefer to use a method like the sheath which they can get over the shop counter or by mail order.

No contraceptive will work unless it is used. It is useless, when dealing with something which affects a couple's private and personal sexual behaviour, for a doctor or a nurse to say 'You must do this'; in the privacy of their own sexual relationship they will not do so unless they wish it. The doctor and nurse may inform, advise and guide, but it is the individual couple who must choose the method which they feel will work best for them.

Bibliography

Baker, A. A. *Psychiatric Disorders in Obstetrics*. Blackwell Scientific Publications, 1967

Barnes, C. G. *Medical Disorders in Obstetric Practice*. Blackwell Scientific Publications, 1974

Bourne, G. *Pregnancy*. Pan Books, 1975

Cartwright, A. *Parents and Family Planning Services*. Routledge, Kegan Paul, 1970

Cross, V. M. & Hill, E. *The Preterm Baby*. Churchill Livingstone, 1975

Da Cruz, V. & Adams, M. *Baillière's Midwives' Dictionary*. Baillière Tindall, 1976

Department of Health and Social Security. *Present-Day Practice in Infant Feeding*. HMSO, 1974

Department of Health and Social Security. *Report on Confidential Enquiries into Maternal Deaths in England and Wales, 1970–1972*. HMSO, 1975

Garrey, M. M., Govan, A. D. T., Hodge, C. H. & Callander, R. *Obstetrics Illustrated*. Churchill Livingstone, 1974

I P P F. *Family Planning for Nurses and Midwives*. 1971

Keahy, A. J. & Morgan, D. M. *Craig's Care of the Newly Born Infant*. Churchill Livingstone, 1974

Law, B. *Family Planning in Nursing*. Crosby Lockwood, 1973

Law, R. G. & Friedman, M. *Midwifery*. Staples Press, 1972

Moir, D. D. *Pain Relief in Labour*. Churchill Livingstone, 1971

Montgomery, E. *At Your Best for Birth and Later*. J. Wright & Sons, 1969

Myles, M. *Textbook for Midwives*. Churchill Livingstone, 1975

Parsons, B. *Expectant Fathers*. Robert Yeatman, 1975

Peel, J. & Potts, M. *Textbook of Contraceptive Practice*. Cambridge University Press, 1969

Rathbone, B. *Focus on New Mothers*. Royal College of Nursing, 1973

Towler, J. & Butler-Manuel, R. *Modern Obstetrics for Student Midwives*. Lloyd-Luke, 1975

Vulliamy, D. G. *The Newborn Child*. Churchill Livingstone, 1972

Glossary of Some Common Terms Used in Obstetrics

Abortion Expulsion of the products of conception from the uterus before the 28th week of pregnancy, when the fetus shows no sign of life.

Acidosis Lowering of the normal alkalinity of the blood below a pH of 7·4 (see pH).

Amniocentesis Withdrawal of amniotic fluid from the uterus via the anterior abdominal wall using a syringe and needle.

Analgesia Loss of sensitivity to pain.

Analgesic drug An agent capable of causing analgesia.

Anencephalic A gross congenital malformation in which the vault of the skull is missing and the brain fails to develop.

Antibody A protein produced in the body in response to the introduction of an antigen. This antibody will only react with the antigen which has caused its production, e g Rhesus antibody will only haemolyse Rhesus positive red blood corpuscles.

Antigen A substance which stimulates the production of an antibody.

Bilirubin A bright yellow bile pigment. An excess of bilirubin stains the skin and tissues yellow, a condition known as jaundice.

Caput succedaneum. An oedematous swelling on the presenting part (usually the head) of the baby which is present at birth but subsides within 24 hours.

Cephalhaematoma A haematoma between the skull bone and its periosteum, caused by the rupture of small blood vessels, due to friction between the head and pelvis in labour. As the periosteum is adherent to the edges of the skull bones, the swelling is confined to one bone. It tends to increase in size for a day or two and then takes several weeks to be absorbed. No treatment is necessary.

Chromosomes Small threads of nuclear material carrying genes which transmit inherited characteristics.

Colostrum Fluid secreted by the breasts from about the 16th week of pregnancy and for the first three or four days after delivery until milk is produced.

Congenital Existing at birth (applied to a condition, usually a malformation).

Cyesis Pregnancy.

Cystic fibrosis Congenital abnormality of the mucus-secreting glands throughout the body. In the newborn this results in dry, bulky, mucoid meconium which may cause intestinal obstruction.

Cytology The study of tissue cells. Cervical cells are examined to detect early carcinoma. Fetal cells in the amniotic fluid can be examined to determine the sex, maturity and some chromosomal abnormalities, e g Down's syndrome.

Down's syndrome (Mongolism) A group of abnormalities including mental subnormality, due to the presence of an extra chromosome. Older women (especially those over 40 years) are more likely to produce a mongol child.

Dystocia Difficult labour.

Eutocia Normal labour.

Gestation Pregnancy.

Gestational age Duration of intra-uterine life.

Gravid Pregnant.

Gravida A pregnant woman.

Hydrocephalus Excess cerebro-spinal fluid distending the ventricles of the brain. The main cause is some obstruction in the cerebro-spinal pathway.

Hypoxia Lack of oxygen.

Infant mortality rate The number of infant deaths during the first year of life per thousand live births per annum. In 1974 the infant mortality rate in England and Wales was 16·3 per 1 000 live births.

Infertility The inability of a woman to conceive (although the cause may be in either the man or the woman).

Infection An invasion of the body tissues by pathogenic organisms.

Involution The return of the uterus to its pre-gravid state during the 6 to 8 weeks following labour or abortion.

Jaundice Yellow discolouration of the skin and mucous membranes caused by an excess of bile pigments in the blood and tissues.

Kernicterus Yellow staining of the basal brain cells caused by severe jaundice in infants, which may lead to serious neurological damage or death.

Ketosis An accumulation of ketone bodies in the blood and urine resulting from incomplete fat metabolism.

Lanugo The fine hair which covers the fetal skin in utero, but which has mostly disappeared by term.

Malposition A term used to describe occipito-posterior positions, when the occiput occupies a posterior, rather than an anterior, part of the pelvis.

Malpresentation Any presentation of the fetus other than the normal vertex, e g breech, face, brow or shoulder.

Maternal mortality rate The number of deaths due to pregnancy or childbearing per thousand registered births in a year. In 1974 the maternal mortality rate was 0·12, including deaths due to abortion.

Meconium A substance which collects in the fetal intestinal tract from about the 16th week of pregnancy and is expelled from the bowel during the first day or two of life.

Meiosis The reduction of the number of chromosomes in a germ cell which follows two consecutive divisions of the nucleus which occur during development.

Moulding A change in shape of the fetal skull due to pressure of the pelvis and surrounding tissues in labour; this process is possible because the bones of the vault of the skull overlap at the sutures.

Multigravida A pregnant woman who has previously had one or more pregnancies.

Multipara A woman who has had more than one child.

Neonatal mortality rate The number of babies who die within 28 days of birth per 1 000 live births per annum. In 1974 the neonatal mortality rate was 10·9 per 1 000 live births.

Neonatal period The first 28 days of life.

Nullipara A woman who has not given birth to a child.

Oligohydramnios A deficiency in the amount of amniotic fluid in the uterus.

Oxytocin A hormone secreted by the posterior pituitary gland which causes the uterine muscle to contract.

Oxytocic drugs Drugs which stimulate the uterine muscle to contract.

Parity Having given birth to a child.

Percentile A point on a frequency scale above and below

which fall a certain percentage of the observations, e g a percentile of 10 means that 90 per cent. of the observations are higher and only 10 per cent. are lower in the set of observations.

Perinatal mortality rate The number of stillbirths and babies who die in the first week of life per 1 000 registered total births in the year. In 1974 the perinatal mortality rate was 20·3 per 1 000 total births.

pH A symbol used to denote the degree of alkalinity or acidity of a solution. A neutral solution has a pH value of 7; a pH above 7 denotes increased alkalinity, below 7 increased acidity.

Phenylketonuria An hereditary condition in which there is a deficiency of the enzyme necessary for the metabolism of the amino-acid phenylalanine. It results in a raised level of phenylalanine in the blood and will lead to severe mental retardation unless early treatment is started. Diagnosed by blood tests (Guthrie or Scriver), or urine test.

Polyhydramnios An excessive amount of amniotic fluid in the uterus.

Pregnancy The period from conception to the delivery of the baby. Normal duration is 280 days, 40 weeks, or 9 calendar months plus 7 days, counted from the first day of the last normal menstrual period.

Primigravida A woman who is pregnant for the first time.

Primipara A woman who has given birth to her first child.

Proteinuria Presence of protein in the urine.

Pseudocyesis Phantom pregnancy. The woman has signs and symptoms which simulate pregnancy but is not pregnant.

Rhesus factor An antigen attached to the red blood corpuscles of 85 per cent. of the population in Europe. Thus 85 per cent. with this antigen in their blood are Rhesus positive; the 15 per cent. without it are Rhesus negative.

Sickle cell disease Abnormal haemoglobins S and/or C may be found in people who originate from Central and West Africa and parts of Asia. It is an inherited condition. The erythrocytes are misshapen (sickle-shaped) and have a very short life span, hence severe anaemia ensues. Condition becomes worse in times of stress such as pregnancy or if the patient requires an anaesthetic or a blood transfusion.

Solute load A term for the concentration of soluble substances, especially electrolytes, delivered to the kidneys. Solute load is higher in artificially fed than in breast fed babies.

Stillbirth The birth of a baby after the 28th week of pregnancy who does not breathe or show any other sign of life after complete expulsion from his mother. The stillbirth rate was 11·3 per 1 000 total births in 1974.

Subinvolution Delayed or incomplete return of the uterus to its pre-gravid state during the puerperium.

Supine hypotensive syndrome A condition in which the blood pressure falls when the patient lies on her back because the weight of the pregnant uterus compresses the inferior vena cava, thereby impeding the return of blood to the heart. The patient feels faint but will soon recover if she is turned on her side immediately.

Système International d'Unités (SI Units) A system of scientific measurements which has been agreed internationally, now being introduced in medical measurements.

Thalassaemia A condition in which an abnormal haemoglobin is found in people of Mediterranean origin. The erythrocytes have a shortened life span, leading to the development of anaemia.

Ultrasound The name given to sound waves with a frequency above that of the human ear. If sound waves of high frequency are directed through the body, they are reflected at any interface (boundary) between tissues. Used as a diagnostic aid in obstetrics.

Vernix caseosa A greasy film which covers the fetal skin in utero to protect it from the amniotic fluid. Has mostly disappeared at term.

Version The turning of the fetus in utero from one presentation to another. External version is carried out by abdominal manipulation. When the head of the fetus is made to present, it is called external cephalic version.

Vertex The area of the fetal skull bounded in front by the anterior fontanelle, behind by the posterior fontanelle and laterally by the parietal eminences.

Index

ABDOMINAL EXAMINATION, 65–67
Abortion, 136, *179*
Abruptio placentae, 137, 139–140
Acidosis, 121, 157, *179*
After-pains, 97
Amenorrhoea, 27, *48*, 54
Amniocentesis, 125, *179*
Amnion, amniotic fluid, 36, 37, *38–40*
Anaemia, 51, 119–120, *143–144*
Analgesia and anaesthesia, 60, 77–78, 162
Anencephaly, 151, *179*
Ante-natal care, 56–69
Anti-D Immunoglobulin, 125
Ante-partum haemorrhage, 137–140
Antibodies, *179*
  Rhesus, 61, *124*, 125
  rubella, 61
Apgar score, *88*, 120
Artificial feeding, 108–109, *111–114*
Asphyxia at birth, 120–121
Asymptomatic bacteriuria, 60, 144
Attitude, 64, 65
Auscultation, 67
BABY, BATHING, 106–107
  care at birth, 87–90
  complications, neonatal, 115–129
  examination of, 90, *102–105*
  feeding, 108–114
  physiology of, 100–102
  stools of newborn, 107
  weight and measurements of, 90, 101–102
Backache, 7, 53, 70, *131*, 147, 148
Ballottement, 66
  internal, 55
Barlow's test, 105–106
Bartholin's glands, 15
Bilirubin, 101, *123*, 125–126
Bi-manual compression, 159
Blastocyst, 32
Blood, changes in pregnancy, 51
  pressure in pregnancy, 51, 59
  tests in pregnancy, 61
Bonding, *see* mother/baby relationship
Braxton Hicks contractions, 50, 55

Breast, anatomy of, 28–30
  ante-natal care of, 67–69
  changes in pregnancy, 50–51
  changes in the puerperium, 93
  engorgement of, 166
  feeding, 90, *108–111*
  milk, constituents of, 112
    formation of, 30
    quantity of, 165–166
  physiology of lactation, 30
  post-natal care of, 97
Breech presentation, 148–151
Brow presentation, 148, *152*
Brown fat, 100
Buccal pitocin, 154
Buttocks, care of baby's, 107, 127
CAESAREAN SECTION, 161–162
Caput succedaneum, 103, *179*
Cardiac disease in pregnancy, 145
Cephalhaematoma, 103, *179*
Cephalometry, 133
Cephalo-pelvic disproportion, 152–153
Cervical cytology, 60, 180
Cervical lesions, 136, 138
Cervix, anatomy of, 19
  changes in pregnancy, 49–50
  dilatation of, 71, 79, 81
  effacement of, 50, 71
Chloasma, 53
Chorion, 35, 40
Chorionic gonadotrophin, 33, *38*, 55, 130
Chorionic villi, 34–35, 37
Chromosomes, 31, *179*
Circulation, changes in pregnancy, 51
  changes in puerperium, 93
  fetal, 41–43
Colostrum, 51, 68, 101, *112*, *179*
Confinement, home, 2, 56–57
Congenital dislocation of the hips, 104, 105–106
Conjunctival haemorrhage, 103
Constipation, 52, 130
Constriction ring, 159–160
Contraception, 168–176
Contracted pelvis, 58, 153
Contractions, *see* Uterine C.
Coombs' test, 125
Corpus luteum, 24, 26, *33*, 53
Crowning of head, 80, 83
Cystic fibrosis, 105, 180
Cytotrophoblast, 33

183

DECIDUA, FORMATION OF, 33
Deep transverse arrest, 148
Deep vein thrombosis, 166
Delivery of the baby, 83–84, 160
Denominator, 65
Depression, 94, 163, 167
Dexamethazone, 121
Diabetes mellitus, 146
Diet, 61, 74, 162
Disproportion, *see* cephalo-pelvic disproportion
Doderlein's bacilli, 16
Down's syndrome, 103, *180*
Drugs given in labour, 77
Ductus arteriosus, 42–43
Ductus venosus, 41–42
ECLAMPSIA, 134–135
Ectodermal cells, 36
Ectopic pregnancy, 136
Embolism, pulmonary, 167
Embryo, 35–36
Emergency obstetric unit, 2
Endocrine system, 53, 94
Endodermal cells, 36
Endometrium, 19, 26–28, 48
Engagement of the head, 65–66, 67, 152–153
Entonox, 77
Episiotomy, *13*, 83
Epstein's pearls, 103
Examination, 65–67, 79
Exchange transfusion, 123, *126*
Expected date of delivery, 48, 57
External cephalic version, 150
Eyes, 83, 103, 106, 127
FACE PRESENTATION, 148, *151–152*
Fallopian (Uterine) tube, 20–22
Family planning, 168–176
Feeding, 108–114
Fertilization, 31
Fetal blood sampling, 76, 157
Fetal circulation, 41–43
Fetal distress, 156–157
Fetal growth, 66, 133
Fetal heart, 67, 75–76
Fetal movements, 54, 55, 57–58
Fetal skull, anatomy of, 43–47
Follicular stimulating hormone, 23
Foramen ovale, 41–42
Forceps delivery, 160
Fundal height, 49, 66, 96
Fundus, 18, 19
GASTRO-ENTERITIS, 128
Genital tract infection, 163
Genitalia, external, 14–15

Glycosuria, 52, 60
Gonorrhoea, 131
Guthrie test, 105
Gynaecoid pelvis, 4–11
HAEMODILUTION, 51
Haemoglobin, 61, 101, 144
Haemorrhoids, 131
Head circumferences, 102
Health visitor, 3, 99
Heartburn 52, 130–131
Hegar's sign, 54–55
Human chorionic gonadotrophin, 33, *38*, 55, 130
Human placental lactogen, 38, 133
Hydatidiform mole, 136
Hydrocephalus, 180
Hydrops fetalis, 124
Hyperemesis gravidarum, 130
Hypernatraemia, 112
Hypocalcaemia, 122–123
Hypofibrinogenaemia, 140
Hypogastric arteries, 42–43
Hypoglycaemia, 119, *122*
Hypothermia, 87, 100–101, 106
Hypoxia, 120–121, 156–157 180
ILIUM, 5
Implantation bleeding, 33, 136
Incontinence of urine, 164
Incubator, temperature of, 118
Infant mortality rate, 1, 180
Infarcts, placental, 39
Infection, maternal prevention of, in labour, 74–75
   in the puerperium, 96–97
   puerpural, 163–164
Infection, neonatal, 126–129
   immunity to, 102
   prevention of, *107–108*, 109, 119
Inner cell mass, 32, 33, *35–36*
Innominate bone, 4–5
Intra-uterine transfusion, 125
Involution, *91–92*, 180
Iron therapy 51, *61*, 144
Ischium, 5
Isthmus, 19, 48
JAUNDICE, 123–126
KERNICTERUS, 123, 126, *180*
Ketone bodies, 60, 181
Kleihauer test, 125
LABOUR, 70–86
   active management of, 148, 155–156
   admission in, 72–73
   complications of, 147–162
   induction of, 154–155

Labour—*continued*
  mechanism of, 80–81
  nursing care in, 73–75
  observations in, 75–76
  relief of pain in, 76–78
  signs of, 70
  stages of, 70–86
  trial of, 153
Langhan's layer, *see* cytotrophoblast
Lanugo, 102–103, *181*
Leucorrhoea, 62, *131*
Levatores ani muscles, 11–12
Lie of the fetus, 64, 65, 67, 152
Linea nigra, 53
Liquor amnii, 36, 40
Lochia, 92
Lower uterine segment, *19*, 48, 71–72
Luteinizing hormone, 23–24
MALPOSITION, *147*, *181*
Malpresentation, *148*, *181*
Mastitis, 104, 165
Maternity benefits, 62–63
Meconium, *101*, *181*
  stained liquor, 75
  test, 105
Meiosis, 31, *181*
Membranes, 35, 36, 39–40, *155*
  rupture of, 70, 72, 79, 155
Mendelson's syndrome, 162
Meningitis, 129
Menstrual cycle, 26–28
Mesoderm, 34, 36
Micturition, *52*, 54, 130
Milia, 103
Mongolian blue spot, 104
Monilial vaginitis, 131
Montgomery's tubercles, 51
Morning sickness, *see* vomiting
Moro reflex, 105
Mortality rates, 1, *181*, *182*
Morula, 32
Mother/baby relationship, 86, 89, *108*, 120
Moulding, 103, *181*
Myometrium, 19–20, 48
OCCIPITO-POSTERIOR POSITION, *147–148*
Occiput, 44, *45*, 80, 147
Oedema in pregnancy, 51, *132*, 134
Oestriol estimation, 133
Oestrogen, 24–26, 33, 38
Oligohydramnios, *181*
Operative deliveries, 160–162
Operculum, *49*, 50, 72

Ophthalmia neonatorum, 127
Ovaries, *22–26*, 28, 31, 50, 92
Oxygen, 118, 121
Oxytocic drugs, 83, 84, *154–155*, *159*, *181*
Oxytocin, 30, 90, *181*
PALPATION, 66
Parentcraft teaching, 3, *69*, *98–99*
Paronychia, 127
Partograph, 79, 155
Pelvic floor, 11–13
Pelvimetry, 67, 150, 153
Pelvis, 4–11, 53
Pemphigus neonatorum, 127
Penthrane, 77
Percentile, *115*, *181*
Perineal body, 12
Perineum, 13, 83, *97–98*
Phenylketonuria, 105, *182*
Phlebothrombosis, 166
Phototherapy, 123
Pituitary gland, *23–24*, 53
Placenta, abnormalities of, 39
  accreta, 160
  delivery of, 84–86
  development of, 33–35
  functions of, 37–39
  manual removal of, 160
  praevia, 137–139
Placental abruption, 139–140
Placental function tests, 133
Placental insufficiency, 59, *141*
Placental localisation, 139
Planned early transfer, 2, 3
Polarity, 72
Polyhydramnios, *143*, *182*
Position, 64–65
Post-natal examination, 99
Post-natal exercises, 95
Post-partum haemorrhage, 158–159, 164
Pre-eclampsia, 132–134
Pregnancy, bleeding in, 136–140
  diagnosis of, 54–55
  duration of, 48
  management of, 56–69
  minor disorders of, 130–131
  multiple, 141–143
  physiology of, 48–54
  skeletal changes in, 53
Preparation for childbirth, 69, 76–77
Presentation, 65, 66, 67, 152
Presenting part, 80
Pre-term babies, 115–120
Prolactin, *30*, 93
Prostaglandin E₂, 154–155

Proteinuria, 60, 132
Prothrombin, 101
Pseudocyesis, 182
Pseudo-menstruation, 104
Puerperium, immediate care, 86–87
  management of, 94–99
  physiology of, 91–94
Puerpural psychosis, 167
Pustules, 127
Pyelonephritis, 144
QUICKENING, 54
REFLEXES OF NEWBORN, 104–105
Renal changes in pregnancy, 52
Respiration, 51–52 88, 100
Respiratory distress syndrome, 121
Respiratory tract infection, 128–129
Resuscitation of the newborn, 120–121
Retained placenta, 159–160
Retained products of conception, 164
Retrolental fibroplasia, 118, 121
Rhesus incompatability, *124–126*, *182*
Rooming-in, 107, 108
Rubella, 58, 61
SHOW, 49, 70, 72, 79
Sickle cell disease, 61, 144, *182*
Skin, 53–54 127,
Smoking in pregnancy, 59, 141
Solute load, 112, *183*
Spermatozoon, 19, *31*, 170, 172
Stillbirth, *183*
Striæ gravidarum, 53–54, 66
Suminvolution, 163, *183*
Succenturiate lobe, 39
Supine hypotensive syndrome, 78, *183*
Surfactant, *100*, 121
Symphysis pubis, 6, 8, 9
Syncitiotrophoblast, 33
Syntocinon, 154, 159
Syntometrine, 83
TALIPES, 104
Temperature control, 100–101
  in low birth-weight babies, 118
Test-weighing, 111
Thalassaemia, 61, 144, *183*
Thrombo-embolic disorders, 166–167
Thrombophlebitis, 163, *166*
Thrush, oral, 128
  vaginal, 131
Tongue-tie, 103

Trichomonad vaginitis, 131
Trophoblast, 32, 33
Tuberculosis, 59, 109
Twins, 141–143
ULTRASONOGRAPHY (ULTRASOUND), 55, 133, 136, 139, *183*
Umbilical cord, abnormalities of, 41
  anatomy of, 37, *40*, 41, 42
  blood specimens, 123
  care of, 89, 107
  infection of, 127–128
  presentation and prolapse of, 156
Urine tests in pregnancy, 59–60
Urinary changes in pregnancy, 52
Urinary disorders in the puerperium, 164
Urinary tract infection 52, 128, 144, 164
Uterine contractions, normal, 70, 71, 75
  hypertonic, 157
  hypotonic, 159
Uterine growth, 49, 66
Uterine infection, 163–164
Uterine tube (Fallopian), 20–22
Uterus, anatomy of, 17–20
  changes of in pregnancy, 48–50
  changes of in labour, 71–72
  changes of in the puerperium, 91–92
  rupture of, 153, 155
VACUUM EXTRACTION, 161
Vagina, anatomy of, 15–17
  changes in pregnancy, 50
Vaginal discharge, 50, 131
Vaginal examination, 67, 79
Varicose veins, 51, *131*
Vasa praevia, 39, 41
Vellamentous insertion of cord, 41
Vernix caseosa, *102*, *183*
Version, external cephalic, 150, *183*
Vertex, 45, *183*
Vitamin K, 101
Vomiting 52–53, 130
WEIGHT, IN PREGNANCY, 59
  of baby, 101–102
Wharton's jelly, 40, 41
X-RAY PELVIMETRY, *see* PELVIMETRY
X-ray soft tissue, 139
YOLK-SAC, 36
ZYGOTE, 31, 32